I'M HIS MOTHER

JOHN D. MCCRAY

I'M HIS MOTHER

Copyright © 2025 **John D. McCray**

ISBN (Paperback): 979-8-89672-115-4
ISBN (Hardback): 979-8-89672-117-8
ISBN (Ebook): 979-8-89672-116-1

Printed in the United States of America.

PROMINENT
BOOKS
EDGE

5830 E 2nd St, Ste 7000 #9983
Casper, WY 82609
USA

"Dedication"

FIRST AND FOREMOST, I WOULD like to thank God for blessing me with my special talent to be able to write my ninth book. I would like to thank my mom and dad for always encouraging me to do my best in whatever I do in life. I would like to thank my siblings for always supporting me, Lamont, Brian, Shakelia, Tyra and Leana. Thank you for your support. A special thanks to Isiah Lemon, Erica Capers, Matthew Collins, Anitra Hammett, Sylinda F. Johnson, Angela Richburg, Lawanda Samuels, Kevina S. Mouzon, Sharia White, Tangie Armstrong, Rhonda Williams, Elroy Wilson, Ethel Barnett, Linda Smith, Elise Byrd, Artrice N. Singleton and Dana Gaillard. To my friends Lee Pickens and Tyrone Fogle, that are no longer here, thank you for your friendship through the years. Last but not least, I would like to thank my grandparents who are no longer here, the late John and Daisy Carraway and Richard and Ida Mae McCray. Thank you all for your love through the years. You are definitely appreciated.

Chapter 1

Please Watch Him

OM AND I WERE SITTING in the living room watching Wheel of Fortune on TV. That's one of our favorite TV shows, that we've been watching since I was a little girl. Seven-o'clock is Jeopardy and seven-thirty, Wheel of Fortune. "Tammy, you haven't told me about your day at work today," Mom said. "Well it was okay. Those old ladies keep me laughing and on my toes at the nursing home," I said. "I can only imagine," Mom replied.

I've been working at Creative Home Care Nursing Home, since I got out of high school three years ago. I work third shift and take online classes for nursing, because being a nursing assistant is nice, but I want to start making the big bucks that the LPN's and RN's make, so I'm going to school to do that.

Mom and I live together in our three-bedroom house. After my father ran off with one of his girlfriends, we've been each other's support group and helped each other. I thought about getting my own place, but I can't leave my mother here by herself, so I decided to stay and help her out with the bills.

Mom and I finished watching Wheel of Fortune, when the doorbell rang. Mom looked over at me and I did the same. "Are you expecting someone, Tammy?" Mom asked. "No, I'm not. You don't have anyone coming over tonight to see you do you?" I asked. "Child please. I wish a man was coming over to see me tonight," Mom said, laughing. I shook my head, and laughed at Mom's comment as I went to the door.

I peeked out the peephole and saw Shemika and Greg standing there. She was holding her son and my godson Calvin, in her arms. I opened the door to see what they wanted, as if I didn't know. "Hey Tammy," Shemika said, hugging me. I hugged her and hugged Greg as well. "Look Tammy, would you watch Calvin for us? We're going to the movies tonight," Shemika said. "You should've called me ahead of time to ask me that, instead of just coming by here like that," I said. "I know. Please watch him for me," Shemika said.

Calvin was smiling and waving at me and I didn't have the heart to tell Shemika no, since she did have Calvin with her. "Okay, I'll watch him this time," I said, as I took Calvin from her arms. "Wow!" I said. "What's wrong?" Shemika asked. "Normally, I work third shift and on Friday nights so you wouldn't have known that I was off tonight, but I forgot we spoke earlier today and I told you I was off. I swear Shemika, you are definitely a trip," I said.

Shemika started laughing like what she was doing was really funny to her. "I know I should be ashamed but I'll make it up to you," Shemika said, giving me Calvin's diaper bag. "I'll be back around eleven or eleven-thirty," Shemika said. "Okay," I said, as Shemika hugged and kissed Calvin. I don't know why but I had a strange feeling that came over me all of a sudden, that I couldn't shake off. I ignored it and closed the door behind them.

"Hey young man," I said, kissing my one-year-old godson on the cheek. "Hey TeeTee," Calvin said, hugging my neck. I brought Calvin in the living room where Mom was sitting. "Hey," Calvin said, waving his little hand at Mom. "Hey sweetie. Come give me a hug," Mom said, hugging and kissing Calvin on the cheek, as he sat on her lap.

"Where's Shemika going tonight?" Mom asked. "She said she and Greg were going to the movies. I forgot that I talked to Shemika earlier and told her I was off tonight so that's why she popped up here instead of calling to see if I would babysit for her. I guess she knew I couldn't say "no" right in front of Calvin," I said. "I know. I don't know why you let that girl use you like that, Tammy.

I've always known that Shemika was that type of girl. I tried telling you that when you were younger, but you wouldn't listen. Now, I bet you see all that for yourself, huh?" Mom said. "Yes I do," I replied.

Mom is one hundred percent right. She's always told me that Shemika is just like her mother, Ms. Sarah. If Ms. Sarah could find a way to use someone, she was definitely going to do just that. Mom told me how Ms. Sarah would ask Daddy to fix her sink because it was clogged up, and she would ask how much he charged and my father would go over there to fix something alright. Mom said she always had an excuse for why she couldn't pay him after he had already done the work.

Mom put her foot down and told my father he better not go back over there to fix anything else for Ms. Sarah, since she's trying to get free service all the time. Rumor had it that Ms. Sarah was paying my father, just not with actual money. Mom could never prove it but she told my father to stay away from her and her house all together. Mom said she could see that Shemika was going to grow up to be just like her mother, always trying to get something for nothing.

Shemika and I have been friends since we were five years old and were in the same Kindergarten class. I remember two big twin girls, Ella and Della would pick on me every day at recess and Shemika saw what they were doing. Shemika picked up a huge tree branch off the ground and walked over towards the girls that had just pushed me down and told them to leave me alone.

Della, who was the toughest sister, told Shemika to mind her business, and Shemika took that branch and knocked Della in the head with it. Della started screaming and Shemika told Ella and Della they better not ever bother me again, and if they did they would have to deal with her. Shemika and I have been inseparable since that day. I told my father what happened when I got home and that's when my father got me some karate and kickboxing lessons to be able to defend myself. He said he couldn't have his only child walking around getting beat up and bullied and have someone running to my rescue.

Shemika is the life of the party and everyone enjoys being around her. She's always been a beautiful girl, and when she started developing that Coca-Cola bottle shape in eighth grade, that's when every guy in school wanted her. Ms. Sarah didn't care what Shemika and her older sister Abbigail did, just as long as they both finished high school and didn't have any babies.

Shemika finished high school, found a job that she barely goes to but she did get pregnant when we were twenty years old, with Calvin. Ms. Sarah wasn't too upset since Shemika was out of school and actually working, but she made it clear that her pregnancy was on her and that was her responsibility, not hers. Ms. Sarah said she was done raising children.

Shemika got three hundred dollars a month from Calvin's father for child support but he never spent time with Calvin. I guess he couldn't afford to spend time with Calvin, since he is a much older married man. At least that's what Shemika always said about him.

I took off Calvin's coat and hung it up. "Calvin, are you hungry?" I asked. "Yes," Calvin said, nodding his head. I got up and fixed him a sandwich and put it on the table for him. Calvin sat at the table and ate his sandwich.

I looked inside Calvin's diaper bag and saw two pair of pajamas, five pair of pants, five shirts, two pairs of sneakers, some socks and about ten Pampers.

I showed Mom what all Shemika packed in Calvin's bag. "Baby, that's a lot of clothes for Calvin to only be staying for a few hours. It looks like Shemika has left her son off on you," Mom said. "Mom, it looks like that but do you think she would actually do that?" I asked. "Child yes. That girl is just like her mother Sarah, I tell you. Shemika doesn't care about anyone else but herself," Mom replied.

As much as I hated to admit it, I think Mom was right. I think Shemika has actually abandoned Calvin and dropped him off on me. I guess that's why I had that strange feeling when she first hugged and kissed Calvin good-bye. She knew she wasn't coming back to get him.

Chapter 2

Where Are You?

I GAVE CALVIN HIS BATH AND got him ready for bed. Calvin was already falling asleep so I laid him down in my bed. I sat beside him on my bed, just watching this little boy as he slept. I looked at the clock and it was twelve-thirty. Where in the world are Shemika and Greg?

I grabbed my cell phone and started dialing her cell number. I waited and waited but no answer. I hope this girl just put her phone down somewhere and just didn't see me calling her. I know Shemika didn't just up and leave her son on me like that, without a word or a phone call or anything.

I just looked at Calvin's handsome little brown-skinned face, as the tears ran down my face. Here I am, a twenty-one year old female, that wants to get married and have children one day, and can't have them, but you have some mothers like Shemika, who have children and don't do right by them or deserve to be a mother. How do you leave your one-year-old son behind like that with someone? Yes, I'm her best friend and her son's godmother, but you still just don't leave him like that.

I thought about my junior year in high school, when I was seventeen and dating Demerio Oliver. Demerio was so handsome; I met him at a football game that my cousin Dray was playing in. Demerio saw me at the concession stand and offered to buy me some nachos and cheese, and I allowed him to. Demerio and I sat outside while I ate my nachos and we talked the entire time. Demerio went to East Clarendon and I went to Manning High, which were about thirty minutes from each other, but he was staying with his grandmother because his mother was sick.

We were both in the eleventh grade and were madly in love with each other. Demerio would ask his cousin Todd to bring him to my house, when my mom was at work. Demerio took my virginity and a few months later, I found out I was pregnant. My parents went ballistic and they wanted to go upside Demerio's head. Demerio promised he was going to do right by me and was going to step up to the plate and take care of me and the baby.

Demerio started changing and acting stupid on me. Our everyday phone conversations quickly decreased to two to three times a week until eventually it stopped all together. My love for Demerio quickly changed when I found out that he not only had me pregnant, but he had another girl at his school pregnant as well.

I was so upset and I eventually went into a state of depression. I later lost my child and what the doctors told me nearly made me want to give up on life altogether. The doctors told me that my fallopian tubes were severely scarred and damaged due to the miscarriage that I had. After the doctors did several tests on me, they told me that I would never be able to bear any children and if I did get pregnant, there was a possibility that I could lose my life in the process of it, so it was best for me to have a hysterectomy, in order to save my life.

I had two second opinions and each doctor confirmed that my chances of having a child and carrying it to terms was nearly impossible, and I definitely didn't want to die in the process of giving birth, so I accepted it and had the hysterectomy. I had to accept the fact that children just weren't in the cards for me.

I felt like I was cursed and felt like I was being punished for getting pregnant at seventeen and not married, for the reason I couldn't have any children in my entire life. So when I see mothers like Shemika, on drugs, alcoholic, and abusive, I don't have any pity or sympathy for them and wonder why they even had a child in the first place, because they certainly didn't deserve for a child to call them those three letters together, that I would love to hear one day, the word "mom."

It was now two o'clock in the morning and I tried calling Shemika's cell phone again but I didn't get an answer. Where in the world is this girl at? Come get your child. I stood up from beside the bed and leaned over and kissed Calvin on the cheek. I turned the light off and turned on the nightlight I had in my room for him. I didn't want Calvin waking up in a strange place and getting scared.

I kneeled down on my knees to pray.

"Dear God,

I don't know where Shemika and Greg are but she left her one-year-old son here with me and I'm supposed to only be watching him for about three hours, but it's been over six hours now and I haven't heard anything from Shemika. Lord, please let this girl come to her senses and come get her son, because I have to go to work tomorrow. I know Calvin is scared and wondering what in the world is going on.

This is something that Shemika's irresponsible self would do to a friend but not to her only son. I wouldn't think she would do that but with Shemika, there's just no telling. We all need you God and so does little Calvin. God let this girl come to her senses and do it quickly by tomorrow before I have to go to work," Amen.

I got in my bed because having all this going on, was definitely making me sleepy. I just hope everything works out tomorrow before I have to go to work.

Chapter 3

Not A Word

IT'S TEN-O'CLOCK IN THE MORNING and I haven't heard anything from Shemika and Greg. Mom had to go to work this morning and she suggested that I go by Ms. Sarah's house or contact Shemika's sister Abbigail, to see if one of them can keep Calvin until Shemika finally returns. I told Mom I'll do that this morning.

I must have called Shemika about twenty times this morning and still no answer. I think I definitely need to go by Ms. Sarah's house so she could keep Calvin. Calvin isn't a problem at all. I got up and fixed him breakfast and got him ready to start the day. I turned Sesame Street on the TV for him and he sat there just watching that. He's such a sweet quiet little boy and doesn't cause any trouble.

I grabbed my keys off the table and put Calvin in the backseat. I don't even have a car seat to put Calvin in. I sure hope I don't get stopped or anything. I tried calling Ms. Sarah before I just popped up at her house, but she never answered the phone.

I pulled up to Ms. Sarah's place and I swear I didn't want to even get out of the car. Ms. Sarah lives in the projects in some old rundown apartments, in the hood. I swear they should've torn this place down a long time ago. This guy that I went to school with got shot and killed last year, from a drive by shooting. I quickly grabbed Calvin's diaper bag and took Calvin by the hand to Ms. Sarah's apartment. I noticed two old ladies sitting in front of their doors, talking. I waved to them and then knocked on Ms. Sarah's door.

"Who is it?" Ms. Sarah yelled, as she finally came to the door. "It's me, Ms. Sarah. Tamara Martin," I said. "Oh hey Tamara. How are you doing?" Ms. Sarah asked, as she gave me a quick hug, smelling like an entire cigarette ashtray. "Ms. Sarah, I'm looking for Shemika. Shemika and Greg came by my house last night and asked if I would watch Calvin because they were going to the movies, but I never heard back from them.

I've been calling and calling her ever since twelve-o'clock mid-night, but I can't get in touch with her and I have to go to work tonight. Have you heard from her at all?" I asked. "No baby I haven't. You know Shemika might be doing one of her disappearing acts again. I remember she asked me to keep Calvin one time and the girl didn't come back until three months later.

Now Tamara, I don't know if the girl is string out on drugs or hopping from man to man but once your children are grown, you stop asking questions and let them be grown. I can't watch Calvin until Shemika gets back home because I don't know how long that will be. The best thing I can tell you is to keep calling her or see if Abbigail will watch Calvin until Shemika comes back, other than that I can't help you," Ms. Sarah said, closing the door back in my face.

I stood there flabbergasted at Ms. Sarah's response, as she turned her back on her own grandson, with me holding his little hand, and he's looking around, wondering what in the world is going on. "This is your grandson and you closed the door on me like that? How can anyone with a heart do that?" I said to myself. I was so pissed off that I knew if I continued standing here at this woman's door, I'll have a few choice words for her.

"Baby, that's a nasty heifer. How you going to turn your back on your own grandson, like that?" the dark-skinned woman said to the older lady beside her. "You know Sarah has always been something nasty. Baby, I sure hope you find Shemika and if you do, don't watch her son for her anymore," the other lady said.

I put the seat belt on Calvin in the back seat, trying my best not to get upset. How in the world could Shemika do this to her own son, by just abandoning him like that? I guess she thought it was okay to leave Calvin with me, her best friend, than a stranger but she already knew what she was going to do when she first brought him over last night for me to watch him.

I pulled up to Abbigail's job. Abbigail is a department store manager at Wal-Mart. Abbigail and I have never been too friendly with each other but we will at least say hello and bye to one another when we see each other out somewhere. I just hope she knows where her sister is or if she will be willing to keep Calvin until Shemika finally shows up.

Abbigail normally works in the customer service area so I'm praying she's working today over there. I brought Calvin inside with me and went over to the customer service area. "Hey ma'am can I help you?" the young lady asked. "Yes is Abbigail here working today?" I asked. "Yes. Who should I tell her is here to see her?" the young lady asked. "Please tell her Tamara is here," I said. "Okay," the young lady said, going through the double glass doors.

Abbigail came up front. "Hey Tamara. How are you?" Abbigail asked. Abbigail is about four years older than us. She and Shemika have never gotten along growing up but I sure hope she can put her differences aside for her sister to at least take her nephew in.

"Hey Abbigail. Have you heard from Shemika lately?" I asked. "No I haven't, Tamara. You know Shemika and I don't talk like that," Abbigail said. "Yeah, I know but you were my last hope. Shemika and Greg came by last night to ask me to watch Calvin for them to go to the movies. She said they would be back by eleven or eleven-thirty to get Calvin and I haven't spoken or seen them since. I have to go to work tonight and I can't keep Calvin with me," I said.

Abbigail shook her head in an apologetic way. "Tamara, I haven't seen or talked to my sister. Have you been by my mother's place?" She asked. "Yes, but she said she hasn't talked to or seen her either. Your mom said Shemika has done her like that before with asking her to watch Calvin and hasn't come back until three months later," I said.

"Tamara, I hate to say this, Lord knows I hate to say this but you may have to contact the police or Child Protective Services because I don't want to get involved in this. I swear I don't know how in the world you and my sister are even friends because you two are like night and day. You're so sweet and would give the shirt off your back to help someone, but my sister is totally opposite and would never do that for anyone. If anything she would take your shirt and hide it, and act like she didn't do it so you wouldn't have a shirt for yourself, because she definitely wouldn't give you hers.

I hope you find her or at least hear back from her, but I don't want to have anything to do with this." Abbigail came closer and hugged and kissed Calvin and told me to take care and whatever I decided was totally up to me. Abbigail went back in the back, leaving Calvin and I standing there.

I couldn't believe these people. This was Calvin's grandmother and his aunt and they didn't want to take him in. I felt like I had a little stray dog that I found in an alley or something and I was begging people to give him a good home, because I didn't want to just leave him like that without anyone. Shemika has really burned some bridges with her family because no one was willing to help or take in her son, because they didn't want to deal up with her. How sad is that?

Chapter 4

Mom Help Me

I T'S BEEN THREE DAYS NOW since I've seen or heard from Shemika. I told Mom how Ms. Sarah and Abbigail acted and what they said. Mom said that wasn't a surprise about Ms. Sarah because Ms. Sarah is definitely Shemika's mother and they were just alike. Mom said Abbigail was a little different and didn't like to be involved in any foolishness or mess. I could definitely see that. Maybe that's why Abbigail acted like she didn't like me, because she thought maybe Shemika and I were just alike, but that couldn't be further from the truth.

Calvin sat in the living room watching cartoons and laughing, just enjoying being a child. Just the smile on this little boy's face made me want to keep him and not put him in the system with all the other foster kids. I can't imagine giving him up and he ends up in the system in some psychotic, crazy foster home with psychotic parents.

I started making dinner, thinking that spaghetti sounded good. Mom came and sat at the table. "Baby, have you decided what you want to do about Calvin?" Mom asked. "Mom, I don't know. Shemika's mom and sister don't want him around because they don't know if Shemika will ever come back or what she's going to do," I said.

Mom grabbed my hand. "Baby, it's time for you to call the police and you have to involve CPS," Mom said. "You're right Mom, but I have a question?" I asked. "What's that baby?" Mom asked. "Would you help me raise Calvin as my son? I don't want him to be in the system Mom, because there's just no telling what he'll go through there," I said.

"Baby, are you sure that's what you want to do? Calvin isn't a toy that you can pick up and play with for a while and toss aside when you're done, so if you're serious and want my help, then I'll be here to help you. Remember Tammy, you're not raising him as his friend. You'll be raising him as his mother. You will have to be stern with him, even when you don't want to. You will tell him "no" and mean just that, "no." Not change your mind because he's upset with you because you told him he can't do something. You have to learn how to discipline him when he gets out of hand and out of control, because believe me if you don't discipline him the right way, someone else will and it may not be the way you want them to. So if you're going to be a parent then be a parent.

I'll help you as much as I can but baby, this is your responsibility that was thrown off on you. Is it fair? No it's not, but life isn't fair. There's always going to be some things that can switch and change the unexpected and that's what happened. Maybe God laid it on Shemika's heart to give her son to someone who would love him and provide for him because she knew she couldn't. But again baby, I'm done raising children but I will help you as much as I can, if you want to raise Calvin as your own son," Mom said.

I listened to everything Mom said because she was definitely right. Raising a child is a big responsibility and I have to make sure I'm willing and ready to do that. Mom said a child doesn't need a parent as a friend, they need a parent as a mother or a father and I shouldn't step up to that plate unless I'm ready to take on that role.

"Mom, I think I want to do this. I want to try to be Calvin's mother, because I can't bear to see him in the system and watch him get lost or placed in someone's home, who's only thinking about getting a little check from him each month and mistreats him. I wouldn't be able to live with myself, knowing that happened and I didn't try to stop it.

Mom was right, that maybe Shemika knew she wasn't fit to be a mother to Calvin and instead of her abusing him or leaving him in the care of strangers, she wanted to leave him in the care of someone she trusted and someone she knew he loved, and someone that loved him in return.

I felt so much better about the situation after Mom said it that way and that she would be there to help me along the way. Deep down, I don't know if I totally agree with Mom though. I think Shemika would've left Calvin with anyone that would've kept him. She didn't care if it was me or the lady on the corner, as long as she didn't have to do it herself, that was all that mattered to her.

I called the police and told them what happened, and the police came out and took a report and asked me if I wanted to file a missing report. I told them that wasn't my call because I doubt if Shemika was actually missing. She was just gone from around me and from around her son. I gave them Ms. Sarah's number so they could see if she wanted to file for one. Nine times out of ten, Ms. Sarah probably won't file for a missing report either because she doesn't think Shemika is missing.

The police told me to contact Child Protective Services tomorrow and they can grant me temporarily custody, until they decided what to do. The officer said hopefully I would hear back from Shemika by then.

I think the best thing to do is to just raise Calvin as my own son because I've heard too many sad stories about foster care and I refuse to put Calvin in the system, even if his own mother, grandmother, and aunt don't care or want him. My mom and I care and we're going to raise Calvin together.

Chapter 5

A Glow

I<small>T'S BEEN SIX MONTHS NOW</small> since the court granted me temporary custody as Calvin's foster mother. It was so hard for Calvin to first get adjusted to his new home. Some nights he would cry himself to sleep or wake up screaming from a nightmare, scared to go back to sleep. I had to get in bed with him a few times a week and hold my baby and rock him to sleep. I guess he was probably missing Shemika.

I've been calling her about five times a day, still praying she would eventually answer the phone and talk to me or at least let Calvin hear her voice. I haven't heard anything from her or from Greg. It's like they just vanished from the face of the earth. At first I was angry and upset and kept calling but then God told me to stop calling her, because if she hasn't answered by now, she'll never answer and that I should just move on and be the best mother I can be.

I used to bring Calvin to Ms. Sarah's place so she could at least spend some time with him but she always acted like she didn't want him around and eventually she told me to stop bringing him altogether. I would go by Wal-Mart so Abbigail could see Calvin. She always hugged him and gave him five dollars. Abbigail told me there was still no sign of Shemika but she's positive that the girl is fine. Abbigail told me after a month that Shemika's been gone, that Ms. Sarah finally filed a missing report on her.

I know Ms. Sarah said that Shemika has pulled that before and stayed away for three months but that would've driven me crazy, not knowing where my child is and whether or not they're still alive. I know once your child is grown, that doesn't mean you stop caring about them and hoping that they're always safe.

Things have been getting a little hectic with working full-time, doing my online classes, and now being a new mother, but I wouldn't change it for the world. I guess it's the look in Calvin's eyes that makes me continue pushing each and every day for him, realizing that it's not about me anymore, it's about me providing a good life for him. I may not be able to have children of my own in the future, but the job of being Calvin's mother is priceless to me and I wouldn't trade it for anything in the world.

I just got to work and clocked in. I did all my rounds and checked on all the residents, except my very last one, Mrs. Ollie Mae. I walked to her room and she was trying to get up out of bed. "What do you need, Mrs. Ollie Mae?" I asked. "Oh, hey there young lady. Do you mind helping me to the little girl's room?"

Mrs. Ollie Mae asked. "I don't mind at all Mrs. Ollie Mae, but please ring the little buzzer in your room so next time I can help you or someone else can. We don't want you to slip and fall," I said.

"You're right baby, but sometimes I want to try and go by myself," Mrs. Ollie Mae said. "Mrs. Ollie Mae, do you want your son and daughter to get mad at us? They will be downright furious if we let their precious mother fall and hurt herself on this hard floor. You don't want them to get me fired do you?" I asked. "No, I sure don't. But baby, they barely even come visit me anyway," Mrs. Ollie Mae said, rolling her eyes. I shook my head at her comment. "But you're right, I don't want you to get fired due to me falling," Mrs. Ollie Mae said.

Mrs. Ollie Mae is one of the residents here and she is the sweetest little lady. She always would touch my face and tell me how beautiful my dark brown-skin is. I just smiled and told her thank you. Mrs. Ollie Mae has been here for over a year now and a lot of the RN's and CNA's say she's mean and gives them a hard time, but I've never had any problems with her at all. She's often shared with me how her son, daughter and grandchildren, never come by to visit her except her grandson Lane, and how nice it would be to see all the rest of her family. I told her I'm sure they'll be by one day when she least expects them to. Mrs. Ollie Mae told me to not hold my breath waiting for that to happen.

I could definitely see her frustration to be in a place like this and never hardly having any family or friends to come by and see you, when both of your children and grandchildren live no more than fifteen and twenty minutes away. I sure hope I'll never end up in a place like this, because I would never put my mother in a nursing home, unless I can't see any other way to keep her at home with me.

I helped Mrs. Ollie Mae in the restroom and told her I'll be outside and to just call me when she's done. She nodded her head and I closed the door behind me to give her, her privacy. I heard the toilet flush and Mrs. Ollie Mae was washing her hands. I guess she said there's some things she can do for herself so she wants to continue doing it while she still can and I definitely can't blame her on that.

I helped Mrs. Ollie Mae to her recliner in her room. "Tammy, you are such a sweet young lady, I know your parents are very proud of you aren't they?" Mrs. Ollie Mae asked. "Yes they are," I said, referring to my mother, but not my father. After my father left, he left my mother and me as well so my mother is all I have.

"Tammy, they have to be. You're such a beautiful young lady. It's so kind of you to be watching out for an old woman like me," Mrs. Ollie Mae said, smiling. "Mrs. Ollie Mae, stop that you're not old. I just hope when I get your age, I'll look just as beautiful and still able to get around as you do," I said.

Mrs. Ollie Mae just smiled as she started flipping through the channels on her TV. Mrs. Ollie Mae said her children decided to put her in the nursing home after she tried to get something out of the closet and slipped and fell and broke her arm two years ago, so she knew it was time for her to be around people that could come check on her on occasion because she didn't want to die in her house all by herself.

Mrs. Ollie Mae is such a delightful lady and has always shared spiritual things with me. She told me that she was a first lady at First Clarendon Church here in Manning, South Carolina. Mrs. Ollie Mae told me that God used to share more things with her then her own husband and he was the pastor. I laughed at her comment.

"Good night Mrs. Ollie Mae. I'll see you in the morning," I said. "Goodnight young lady and congratulations on your new little boy," Mrs. Ollie Mae said. I quickly turned her light back on and walked back inside her room. "Mrs. Ollie Mae, how do you know I have a new little boy?" I asked. "Baby, I just told you sometimes God shares stuff with me and shows me things as well. I knew there was a reason why you had that beautiful, bright glow around you and I knew someone had to put it there.

Baby, God would show and tell me a lot about our church members and when I told them what God shared with me, they always thought that someone was telling me their business, but it was only God that was showing me things.

Young lady, this little boy is going to bring you so much love in your life, but where there's joy, there is also pain and hurt. You're going to go through some stuff in the next few years, but God is only using you but in the end, when you think the devil just eased up off you, baby it's going to get even worse. People are going to come into your life that should've never been there in the first place but when you realize what they're about, then you'll know the truth and you'll be able to move on.

It's amazing how God has to get you alone by yourself in order for you to see things that are so much clearer to you, after you come through all this, you're going to realize it was nobody but God that brought you through it," Mrs. Ollie Mae said.

Mrs. Ollie Mae's words made a lot of sense, but I just didn't know what it meant but I know God had to be showing her something about me because I never shared anything about Calvin with any of my coworkers or my supervisor. My business would be all over this nursing home and I don't want that.

Chapter 6

Happy Birthday

TODAY IS CALVIN'S FIFTH BIRTHDAY. He kept asking me about his party that I'm having for him today. I invited a few kids over from his class and from church. I was expecting about twenty kids to come over. I invited Ms. Sarah and Abbigail over as well. Ms. Sarah gave me twenty dollars to give him and she told me to tell Calvin happy birthday and she loves him. I guess that meant she wasn't coming to his party.

Abbigail told me she was going to definitely try to come and bring her two children, Brandon and Janitra. They're a little older than Calvin but he enjoys seeing them and spending time with them. Abbigail often tells me what a wonderful job I'm doing raising Calvin and being his mother. I thanked her and told her Calvin used to have lots of nightmares when we first got him, but now he's doing a lot better and those nightmares have finally stopped.

I told Abbigail how Calvin can be a little hardheaded and doesn't like to listen and how I sometimes have to show him the other side of me and tear his other side up. Abbigail laughed and told me that was all in good parenting and she sometimes has to discipline hers everyday, but now since they're getting a little older, she doesn't have to do it as much. Abbigail told me if her mother had just disciplined Shemika more then what she did, then maybe she would've turned out to be a little more responsible and more stable, which I totally agreed with.

Abbigail said Shemika called Ms. Sarah a few months ago to say hello and to say she's doing fine. She told me that Ms. Sarah said Shemika sounded like she was on some kind of drugs or half drunk or something. Abbigail asked if I heard from her. I told her she never called me or anything but she sent me a video to my email, explaining how sorry she was for just vanishing out of Calvin's life like that and just dumping him off on me.

I told Abbigail that I knew she probably would never call because she knew I would go off on her, so I guess she felt an email was the next best thing to do. At first I wondered why Ms. Sarah didn't contact me and tell me she heard from Shemika, but maybe she felt like she didn't have to. But if it was me, I definitely would, especially since I'm raising her son. Ms. Sarah has always been a strange acting woman; I guess that's why Shemika left Calvin with me and not her mother.

Things in my life were starting to change. I met someone that I used to go to school with. His name is Steven Williams. Steven and I did our internship at the same hospital. Steven finished his degree in Radiology and I finished my clinical and finally became a registered nurse.

I had a new degree and now a new man in my life. Steven knows all about Calvin and our situation with how I ended up raising him. I also told him about my situation about me having children and he told me he understood and that he has a little boy so he wasn't interested in having more children, unless I wanted more. Steven said that Calvin and his son Stephan were just enough for him.

Steven asked me to marry him last month and I accepted his proposal. I'm a little skeptical about moving in with him, since it's always been my mom, Calvin and me but now I have a new potential husband. Mom told me to not worry about her because I have to live my own life and she didn't expect me to live with her forever.

I told Mom I would've never been able to get through this without her help or helping me raise Calvin. Mom told me that she was extremely proud of me on how I jumped to the task and became a mother to Calvin. Mom told me she only gave me the guidance on how to do it but everything else, I would learn on my own and I certainly did.

Mom took Calvin out today for his birthday, that way I would be able to decorate the house for his party. I went and got his birthday cake earlier and all his gifts. I told all my guests to park in the back of the house, that way Calvin wouldn't be able to see anyone here.

Calvin knows I'm having a party for him but I don't think he's expecting anyone but just his family. He has no idea that people from his class and church will be here as well.

All the cars finally arrived at the house and everyone parked in the back like I asked. I texted Mom and told her she could bring Calvin home now. My cousin Lamont was on the grill, grilling hotdogs and hamburgers for the party.

Mom texted me and told me she was five minutes away from the house. I went outside and had everyone gathered in the living room to yell out surprise to Calvin. "I'm walking up now," Mom said. "Everyone, they're walking up the driveway now."

I heard the key in the door and Mom pushed Calvin in, and we all jumped out and yelled surprise. Calvin jumped because I knew we scared him and then he burst out laughing. "Ah Mom, you did all this for me?" Calvin asked. "Yes son. It's all for you," I said, smiling.

Calvin had tears in his eyes and I knew this meant a lot to him. My son is quiet and he doesn't like a lot of people around him but he seems to be okay for now with this. Calvin grabbed me around my neck and kissed me on the cheek. "Thanks Mom for my birthday party but next year, I'd rather it just be us," Calvin said laughing. I laughed because I knew Calvin meant those exact words too.

Chapter 7

Getting Settled

I**T'S BEEN A MONTH NOW** since Calvin and I moved in with my new husband Steven. I asked Calvin how he felt about us living with Steven. He seemed okay but he said he was going to miss his grandmother. I told him his grandmother would still be picking him up every day from school and that would be their special time together until I got off from work.

I switched over my shift when I finished nursing school and became a nurse. The hospital wanted me to work there but the nursing home I was working since I was eighteen, wasn't having that so they offered me more money for me to stay there with them. I agreed but told them I had to get off third shift and they allowed me to switch so I could be home with my son and my new husband.

I started moving and placing my things in the house. Steven didn't have anything on the walls, so he told me he didn't care how I decorated the house, as long as I didn't have all kinds of flowers hanging all over the place. I laughed because I told him I didn't like flowers like that.

Calvin helped me straighten his room up and then he sat on the bed like he was tired. "Are you tired, son?" I asked. "I sure am. Moving is a lot of work," Calvin said, like I had him working the entire day or something, knowing he only helped with his room. I just laughed at Calvin's comment.

I got up and went to the kitchen to start making dinner. Mom taught me a lot of new dishes to make instead of what I used to eat. She told me now that I had a son and now a new husband, that I had to start making real meals because no man wants fries, hotdogs and burgers all the time, after a hard day of work.

I agreed and I started watching YouTube and cooking channels, learning how to make certain meals. I decided on meatloaf tonight, which would be my first time making meatloaf so I'm excited to try something new.

I started preparing the meatloaf, while looking on my phone at the cook that was preparing it. I sure hope I don't mess this food up. I placed the pan in the oven with the foil on top and closed the oven door and set it for forty minutes, while I made the rest of the food on top of the stove.

I heard the front door close and I walked around to greet Steven. "Hey baby. How are you?" I asked, giving Steven a hug and a kiss. "I'm okay baby. How are you?" Steven asked. "I'm good. I was just sorting things around and decorating a little," I said. "Oh really?" Steven said, as he looked around in the kitchen and living room. "Okay. It looks quite nice in here baby. Just don't over crowd the walls with a lot of stuff," Steven said. I nodded my head to agree with him.

I guess that's a big difference when having your husband move into your already decorated home, instead of moving into his. You already have your place decorated and know how you want it, but their house is a different story because they know how they want their place as well.

I wanted to suggest some new furniture but I know he probably won't go for that right now, so I'll just leave it at the decorations. I don't want him to think that I got here and just took over everything.

"Baby, it sure smells good in here. What are you making for dinner?" Steven asked. "I'm making meatloaf, green beans, and mashed potatoes," I said. "Okay, that sounds good. Where is Calvin?" Steven asked. "He's in his room, probably watching TV," I said. "Oh okay nice. I think I'll go take a little nap until dinner is ready. Please let me know when you're done cooking," Steven said. "Okay. Are you going to go speak to Calvin before you take your nap?" I asked. "I'll do it later while we're eating," Steven said. "Okay," I replied.

I know Steven isn't Calvin's biological father but he's not going to be ignoring my son, like he's not in the house with us. I want him to spend time with him and teach him how to be a man, things I know I can't do.

We all sat down at the table and blessed our food. Steven said the blessing. "So how are you liking your new room so far Calvin?" Steven asked. "I like it. It's a lot of room in there," Calvin said. "How's your bed? Do you sleep good in it at night?" Steven asked. "Yes sir. It's a nice bed. I like it," Calvin said.

I can tell Steven doesn't have too much experience being around children. His son Stephan came to our wedding but he hasn't been over to stay the weekend yet since we moved in the house. I wonder why is that? Steven said he's a few years older than Calvin but I think that will be good for Calvin to have someone close to his age to play with. I think Stephan is seven or eight.

"Baby, when is Stephan coming over to stay the weekend? I think it will be nice if Calvin and Stephan got to know each other," I said. "I don't know. I'll check with his mom and see if it's okay with her," Steven said. "Okay, sounds good. I would love to get to know my new stepson. Maybe I could take him and Calvin to the park or skating or something," I said. "Okay, well I'll see if that's okay. Maybe this weekend or next weekend," Steven said.

I nodded my head, not wanting to press the issue too much. Steven didn't have much to say after I asked that question. I wonder if there's some deeper reason he doesn't have him like that. I know Calvin and I have only been living here for a month so far but there's no sign that Stephan was ever here at all. Maybe there's something that Steven isn't telling me about the relationship he has with his son or his mother, Steven's ex-girlfriend, Shonda.

Chapter 8

Mrs. Ollie Mae

I JUST DROPPED CALVIN OFF AT school and got to work. I clocked in one minute before I'm considered being late. "Good morning Tamara. I can't believe you're just now getting here? You're always here running around the nursing home, like your head is on fire or something," Casey said. "Good morning to you too," I said, ignoring Casey's comment and grabbing my charts to do my rounds.

Casey is an RN and she took my overnight shift, when they gave me first shift. She said she wanted third shift so she could take her sickly mother to all her doctor's appointments in the daytime. Casey said she's the only child so it falls on her to do everything. She said after her father died, her mother just started going downhill, so she had to move her in with her.

Casey trained me when I first got here but no one gave her the memo that she's no longer training me and needs to watch me like a hawk. I had to go toe to toe with Casey a few times and tell her she's not the boss over me and to get out of my face. Casey is the type that will set you up, to try to get you fired so she could get some brownie points with our Director.

I can't stand working with people like that. I checked on all my residents to make sure they were up and doing well. I was about to check on Mrs. Ollie Mae, when the CNA Amy, came out of her room, almost running me over. "Hey there. Are you okay?" I asked.

Amy shook her head as if she was about to go off or something. "No! That Mrs. Ollie Mae is something else. I tried to help her with her shower and she told me to get out of her room, because she was waiting on the pretty black nurse to help her. I asked her who was she talking about and she said Nurse Tammy. Girl, I hope when I get that old, I'm not that mean that people wouldn't want to deal up with me. So Tamara, she's all yours," Amy said, rolling her eyes and walking off.

I wanted to tell Amy that she's not old and it's hard for people to deal up with her now. I shook my head and knocked on Mrs. Ollie Mae's door, before walking inside. "Good morning Mrs. Ollie Mae. How are you doing this morning?" I asked, giving Mrs. Ollie Mae a hug. "There's my pretty black nurse," Mrs. Ollie Mae said, clapping her hands, as if she was so happy to see me.

I just laughed at Mrs. Ollie Mae because I could tell she was happy to see me and I was just as happy to see her. "So, you wouldn't let Amy give you a shower?" I asked. "No! That young lady is so rough. She doesn't know how to handle an old fragile woman like me. She just started grabbing and pulling and tugging all over me, like I was a piece of rope or something. I told her if she doesn't take her dirty hands off me, I was going to hit her with my cane," Mrs. Ollie Mae said.

I shook my head at Mrs. Ollie Mae. "Now Mrs. Ollie Mae, you know that's not nice to hit anyone with a cane," I said. "I know but she was pissing me off," Mrs. Ollie Mae said. "Well, I'm here to help you. Are you okay with that?" I asked. "I sure am," Mrs. Ollie Mae said, squeezing my hand. "I sure hope your parents know just how lucky they are to have such a wonderful daughter like you," Mrs. Ollie Mae said.

"I think my mother does but my father left my mother, shortly after I turned fifteen, but I'm sure he knows as well," I said. "So tell me how that son of yours is doing? Wait, did you all have a celebration or something? Okay, it was his birthday not long ago?" Mrs. Ollie Mae said. I shook my head, knowing that Mrs. Ollie Mae really does know things because I never told anyone about his birthday party that I had for him and I never told anyone about my marriage, even though I didn't have a big wedding or anything.

I know I shouldn't be sharing my personal business with Mrs. Ollie Mae but sometimes she gives me such good advice and besides that, I'll make it sound like she's delusional if she started repeating anything I told her. "Mrs. Ollie Mae, Calvin is doing good but sometimes it's Steven. Steven sometimes barely says anything to Calvin. I figure that since Calvin is a little boy, he would try bonding and spending some time with him but it's the total opposite. I want a strong male figure in Calvin's life and I thought Steven would be that but it seems he has no interest in bonding with Calvin like that.

I even suggested that he should get his son Stephan for the weekend so they could spend time together, since they're stepbrothers but he almost acted like I offended him when I suggested that," I said. "Okay, well what exactly did he say when you asked him?" Mrs. Ollie Mae asked. "He said he'll ask his mother but I think that was just his way of making me leave it alone," I said.

"Well, looks like you might need to have a conversation with the little boy's mother. I bet she can tell you why your husband doesn't see his son like that," Mrs. Ollie Mae said. "I'm sure she can but I can't go looking for her to ask her something like that. Suppose she goes back and tell Steven and he gets upset with me and that causes problems in our marriage? Mrs. Ollie Mae, I don't want to end up being divorced and I just now got married a month ago," I said.

Mrs. Ollie Mae nodded her head as I helped her dry off out of the shower. "Well sweetheart, if it's something hidden that he doesn't want you to know it will come out one way or the other. The truth has a way of showing its ugly face when we don't want it to.

No matter how hard we try to hide it. I got a feeling his truth isn't anything small at all," Mrs. Ollie Mae said.

I tried not to look so worried but something tells me that Mrs. Ollie Mae is right. I think Steven is hiding something that he doesn't want me to find out about. How in the world do I find out what it is?

If I go snooping around and go looking for Shonda, then it will look like I don't trust my husband and I don't want to do that. Maybe I should leave well enough alone and just hope that Steven will bring the boys together and that he'll be more active in Calvin's life. He's the only male figure that Calvin has right now and Calvin needs that male bonding. That's something I can never give him.

Chapter 9

Shonda

I TEXTED MOM AND ASKED HER if she could keep Calvin a little longer than normal, and forgot to tell her I was getting my hair done. She told me she would be glad to. I got to the hair salon and sat down. "Hey Tamara. I have about thirty more minutes left on Marlene's hair and I'll be right with you," Anita said. "Okay. No problem," I replied.

I grabbed a magazine off the coffee table and started flipping through it. I swear, I don't know why hair stylist and barbers book people at a certain time, knowing darn well they won't be able to see them at that time. Now I have to sit here and wait until Anita is done with her client's hair before she can even start on me. Never mind what I have to do and need to get out of here in a timely manner to do it. I guess if I want my hair done, then I'll just sit here and wait.

I was trying not to look like I was pissed but I couldn't help it. I was so angry, I could walk out of here but I can't go around having my hair looking like this for another day. I saw a crossword puzzle in the magazine and I decided I was going to do it. I took a pen out of my purse and started circling the words that I found.

I looked up when I heard someone come inside the salon. Lord behold, it was Shonda, Steven's ex-girlfriend. I couldn't believe that it was actually her. Mrs. Ollie Mae and I were just talking about her today and Mrs. Ollie Mae told me that I needed to talk to her and now here she is.

The young lady sat beside me but didn't say anything at first. I wanted to reintroduce myself to her since the last time I saw her was at my wedding, but something tells me that Shonda knows exactly who I am.

"Hello," Shonda said. "Hello Shonda. How are you?" I asked. "Wow, so you remember me huh?" Shonda asked. "Well, it's only been a little over a month," I said, laughing. Shonda laughed as well. "Look Tamara, we need to talk. I don't want to sound like a jealous ex-girlfriend but I just want you to be careful with Steven," Shonda said. "What do you mean, be careful?" I asked. "You don't really know Steven like I do. He has a terrible temper," Shonda said.

I looked at Shonda and she was actually trembling, like she was afraid or something. "What do you mean Shonda?" I asked. "He's extremely jealous. Does he know you're getting your hair done?" Shonda asked. "No, he doesn't," I replied. "Okay call or text him now, because he's going to go ballistic when you come home and your hair is done. Steven is going to swear you were out there doing something with someone. When you get home and he starts questioning you and giving you the third degree, don't say I didn't warn you," Shonda said.

I listened to what Shonda was saying but after two years of us dating, I haven't seen that side of him. I do remember that this guy accidentally walked into me, when he wasn't paying attention and on his phone. Steven wanted to bash the guy's head in. I kind of thought the guy deserved that because he was a jerk about it and Steven wasn't up for his foolishness.

Steven made the guy apologize and told him what would happen if he ever disrespected him or me again. The guy took off in his truck in a hurry. Steven kept apologizing to me and told me he didn't mean to carry on like that and he just lost it when the guy acted so nonchalant, like it was no big deal. I told Steven it was okay and that he only defended my honor.

"Shonda, I don't know whether I believe this or not," I said. "Well Tamara, I'm not trying to make you believe me, I just thought I should tell you. I promise you, you don't have to believe me because if you're out past the time he gets home from work, you'll see exactly what I'm talking about.

The only reason why I'm warning you is that you have a son and he could accidentally flip on him. Tamara, Steven is bipolar and schizophrenic. Do you want to know how I found out? One day I spent the night with Steven, when he didn't know I was coming over. He let me in the house. We were asleep in the bed and I got up and went to the kitchen to get some water because I was extremely thirsty.

When I went in the kitchen, he had his medication on the kitchen counter. The medication was called Risperidone and some other medication that started with a "Q". I grabbed my phone off the living room table and looked up the name of the medication and when I saw it was for bipolar and schizophrenic patients, I immediately panicked and had an uneasy feeling in the pit of my stomach.

When I turned around after I Googled it, Steven was standing right behind me. Steven asked me what was I doing in the kitchen and holding my phone in my hand, along with his bottle of medication. I told him I saw it on the counter and I was just curious of what he was taking. Steven hauled off and slapped me so hard, that I thought he took the side of my face off.

Steven then punched me in my stomach so hard, that I fell on the floor. Tamara, to be honest I don't know how in the world I got out of his apartment alive but I did. I ended up pulling a butcher knife out on him and grabbed my things and left.

I called the police and told them what happened and the police arrested Steven. Steven must have got that expunged off his record because he was able to work at that hospital as a doctor. So look Tamara, believe me or don't believe me, that's your choice but all I ask is that you be careful and when he flips on you like I promise you he's going to do tonight after you come home after him, then you get your son and get the hell out of there.

Shonda grabbed my arm, still trembling with fear. You know why my son can't go anywhere around his father or come to your house?" Shonda asked. "Why?" I asked. "Because my son is in a lockdown facility where he is treated for his mental illness. I knew something was wrong with Stephan when he would do the strangest things like take his hand or finger and put it in hot scalding, boiling water, or would cut himself with a knife from his hand to his elbow and have blood all over the place and he would just laugh about it like it was funny.

Tamara, it was so bad that I had to lock my son in his room at night as well as myself in my bedroom, because I was terrified of what he might do. You have no idea what it feels like to fear your own child.

I wish someone had told me all this before I had a child by Steven but then again, I wouldn't believe them. I mean look at him. How can someone as fine as Steven is, be so messed up in the head? Trust me girl, being fine and good at sex is nothing when you don't know if you're going to wake up beside Dr. Jekyll and Mr. Hyde, in the morning or someone standing over you with a knife, trying to kill you.

Tamara, you don't know if you're going to go to sleep and wake up, surrounded by a house with flames all around you or Steven holding a gun on you. If anything happens to you or your son, please don't say I didn't warn you.

Tamara, I have one thing to ask of you to please not tell Steven that you spoke to me and I told you anything about this because he'll definitely come bothering me and I'll have to kill that fool," Shonda said.

"I won't. I promise you, I'll never do that. But Shonda, what proof do you have that I can follow up to check out what you're telling me? I can't just take your word for it," I said. "Trust me, like I said come home after he does tonight and you'll see for yourself and there's one person that I know that will tell you the truth, and that's his grandmother Mrs. Lucille Gibbons. Mrs. Lucille lives in Gable in an old white board house. Here's her address," Shonda said, reaching in her purse and grabbing a pen and piece of paper.

Shonda wrote Mrs. Lucille's address down on the paper and handed it to me. Look Tamara, there's one more thing I know to tell you. There's a cabinet close to the sink in the corner. There's a white and black jar in there. That's where he keeps all his medication bottles at but he keeps a few for that week in that seven-day medication pill box, so you can't see the name of what he's taking. So if you want proof, look in that top cabinet in that jar at his medication and go visit Mrs. Lucille. That's your proof right there. Look, take care of yourself and your son," Shonda said, grabbing my hand and then getting up and hurrying up out of the salon.

After Shonda left, I definitely didn't want to believe her but the way that woman was acting and trembling, she was definitely afraid of Steven. She was afraid of what Steven might do if he was to find out that she talked to me and tried to warn me about him. I'm definitely not going to lie; I was afraid like I've never been afraid before in my entire life.

Chapter 10

SATAN

I PICKED CALVIN UP FROM MOM's house and headed home. Steven called me about five times asking where I was. After I was done talking to Shonda earlier, I texted Steven and told him I was getting my hair done and I might be getting home closer to eight-thirty or nine-o'clock. Steven didn't respond at the moment but started hitting me up and calling me like crazy when I got in Anita's chair.

I answered my phone and told him I was just getting in the chair to get my hair done and couldn't talk at the moment and then I had to hang up. It was already like seven-ten by the time Anita got to me. Steven acted like he had a little attitude but I texted him earlier and told him where I was, so it wasn't like I didn't let him know.

Shonda told me when we talked if I got home later than Steven, I'll see just how crazy he is. I swear if Steven puts his hands on me, that fool will see how crazy I am. The last thing I'm going to be is someone's punching bag, that they think they can take their frustration out on me because they had a bad day at work or someone pissed them off in the grocery store or something.

Calvin wasn't saying much in the car. I looked in the rearview mirror and he was knocked out. I just smiled, I guess my baby had a long day at the park and they got hotdogs for dinner and ice cream later. I know he enjoyed that.

I pulled into our driveway and told Calvin to wake up. Calvin grabbed his things and we walked in the house. Steven was sitting in the den, with the TV on. "Hey baby," I said, walking over towards him. "Don't you hey baby me! It's nine-thirty, where the hell have you been?" Steven yelled, jumping up off the couch. "First of all, I'm going to need you to not talk to me like that and lower your voice. I'm not your child," I said.

Steven walked up towards me with an evil look in his eyes as if he was possessed or something. I knew that the way he was looking and acting that Shonda wasn't lying about him. She was telling me the truth, but I guess I had to find out for myself and something tells me, I'm about to find out everything tonight and right now.

Calvin was looking scared, standing by me. "Sweetheart, go put on your pajamas and get in the bed. Don't come out here for anything okay?" I said. "Okay Mommy," Calvin said, walking towards his room.

"Look Steven, I texted you and told you I was getting my hair done and I didn't expect to get out so late but I did. It's not like you didn't know where I was," I said. "You think I'm stupid don't you? You don't think I know what's going on? You out here messing around on me with someone else aren't you?" Steven yelled. "Please Steven, we're only been married for a little over a month now. Why would I be messing around with someone else?" I said, walking off.

"Don't walk away from me when I'm talking to you," Steven yelled, grabbing my arm like I'm some five-year-old child. I snatched away from Steven. Something tells me that I'm going to have to use my karate, kickboxing, martial arts training, my dad had me take as a child, when I started having problems with Ella and Della back then. I had to defend myself against those two bullies and it looks like I'm going to have to defend myself against my own husband as well. "Okay Steven, let's not do this," I said, to myself, as I pushed him off of me.

Steven stumbled back, almost falling but he didn't. He ran up on me, like he was about to tackle me on a football field or something. I jumped out of the way and kicked him dead in the stomach. Now I know I'm no match for Steven, I'm only 5'7", one hundred and fifty-seven pounds and Steven is 5'10", and one hundred and eighty pounds. I'm not saying I can beat him up but I know how to keep his big rusty behind up off of me. I promise him, a sister is definitely going to fight back.

Steven grabbed his stomach after that kick, like he was shocked that I kicked him. "You kicked me!" Steven yelled, walking up on me. "Only because you grabbed me. I'm your wife and you're my husband. I'm supposed to respect you and you're supposed to respect me. You will not put your hands on me and think I'm going to sit here and let you. I'm no one's fool or punching bag and I'm not your punching bag!" I yelled.

"Tell me, who you're seeing? Tell me your boyfriend's name? Who is it? Who is it Tamara?" Steven yelled, as if he wanted a name and he didn't care whose name I yelled out, as long as it was a name.

"Steven you're crazy. I'm not seeing anyone. I love you and only you. Please stop this!" I shouted. Steven grabbed me by my neck, trying to choke the life out of me, and I did a technique I learned in one of my defense kickboxing classes. "Trying to Survive, Whatever Means Necessary," and this was that time to do everything that I learned.

I turned to the side and dropped down and as soon as Steven tried to come down with me, I took my arm and gave him an uppercut to the groin area. Steven fell on the floor screaming, and holding himself. I ran to the kitchen and picked up a bar stool and I started beating him with it.

I started hitting him and hitting him, and hitting him, until I lost myself in the moment. I felt like Jennifer Lopez in the movie "Enough" when she was kicking her husband's behind at the end, when she was fighting for her life and she survived because she knew she had enough and a child she had to raise.

I finally stopped hitting Steven and called the police and told the police that my husband jumped on me and attacked me. The police arrived in about ten minutes. I opened the door as the officers ran inside. Steven was still lying on the floor, with his eyes open.

"Ma'am, I thought you said, your husband attacked you," The male officer said. "He did, I just fought back and with me fighting back, he just couldn't take my licks like how he was dishing them out to me," I said.

The female officer burst out laughing. "Hell yeah! I know that's right. My girl said she fought back and he just couldn't take her licks like how he was dishing them out," the officer said, clapping her hand and acting like what I said, was the funniest thing to her.

"Ma'am, I can't tell you how many calls we get each and every night about a husband or boyfriend, that jumped on his wife or girlfriend and beat her up, really badly. Most women look like they just got out of a boxing ring, with Mike Tyson and the husband is standing all tall, without a scratch on him, and he's looking like he just did something he should be proud of. The man had the audacity to be looking at us, like he has no idea why we're there to arrest him, but I can see that's definitely not the case here. I wish a lot of women learned how to fight back like you've learned, because a few might still be alive today if they did. I don't know what you're planning on doing after this but I hope you learn if he hits you once, then most likely, he'll do it again.

How long have you two been married?" the officer asked. "About a month and a few weeks," I said. "Oh my God, you two haven't been married long at all. Sweetheart, that's a sign right there. If he starts hitting you this soon in your marriage and you haven't been married long, trust me, this won't be his last time he's going to try and put his hands on you. I'm not telling you to leave him, because that's your decision and your decision alone. You just better be careful what you allow because the next time it might not be a next time," the officer said, as they walked Steven to their car in handcuffs.

The female officer's words really stood out to me. I can only imagine how many women wanted to get out of their abusive marriage or relationship and they always said, I'm going to give him one more chance and then another chance and now they're finally out of chances. I won't allow myself to go through that. I will not leave my son behind without a mother, since his own biological mother abandoned him and never looked back. I'm done and so is my month and a few weeks' marriage. Satan has no place in our marriage and definitely not with me.

Chapter 11

This Is Always Your Home

PACKED UP ALL OUR THINGS and put them in the car. I called Mom and told her what just happened and she told me to come home. I got Calvin and had him lying on the couch. I was about to walk out of the house until I remembered what Shonda said about Steven's medication and where he had it stored.

I quickly grabbed a chair and stood on it so I could look in the cabinet for the jar. I found the black and white jar that Shonda described to me and I opened it. I saw all the bottles of medication that Steven had. I grabbed my phone and took a picture of the front description of the bottles and kept it in my phone. I wanted to take a picture so I could Google it later on. I put the medication back in the jar and placed it back where Steven had it.

As I was driving back to my mother's house, I started crying. I couldn't stop my tears because why didn't I see this type of behavior from Steven before in the entire two years of us dating? There were no signs that he could be violent, other than that guy that bumped up into me that was too busy on his phone. It wasn't like I was afraid that Steven was going to hurt him or anything, he just put him in his place but now I'm afraid of him.

I can't be with someone that I'm afraid of, not knowing whether they're going to just pop off on me. Like the officer said, if he could do this after us being married for only one month, imagine what I'll have to endure through the rest of our marriage if we stay together.

I grabbed our things out of the car and brought them inside the house. Mom came out and helped me as well. I grabbed Calvin and put him in his old bed. Calvin turned over, like he was right at home. I guess he always thought of Mom's house as his home. I leaned over and kissed him on the forehead and turned the light switch off but turned the nightlight on in his room.

I looked up at the clock and saw it was eleven-thirty. I sat down on the couch across from Mom. "Baby, you look like you went through hell and back. What in the world is wrong with Steven? Why would he do something like that?" Mom asked. "Mom, I went to get my hair done and I texted him and told him where I would be and how long it would probably take. I told him I may not get in until late about eight or nine-o'clock.

When I got home, Steven came in my face, acting like I was out cheating on him. He kept asking me who was I with and where was I? He started putting his hands on me, like he was my father or something. I may look small but you know big things come in small packages and I was ready to go to him when he grabbed me. I'm so glad that Daddy made sure I took all kinds of training lessons on how to defend myself.

I'm glad Mr. Gates taught us how to fight a man, especially bigger than us, well at least how to get him off of you. Mom, while I was hitting Steven with the stool, I had no idea what happened to me. It was like, I was trying to kill him or something," I said.

"Baby, I think you were trying to kill what you thought was inside of him. You might have seen a demon or something and you were trying to beat that out of him," Mom said. I don't know if that's what I saw but I was beating the hell out of something and at that time, I saw him. The one I took vows with and shared my body with in intimate moments of our marriage, in and out of the bedroom.

He acted like he wanted me dead and I acted like I wanted him dead. At that moment, it was me or him and I was determined to come out on top," I said. "Well, I'm glad you did but baby, are you planning on going back to him?" Mom asked. "No I'm done!" I said.

"Well baby, it's your life and if you choose to go back to him then I won't say anything against that but just my opinion. The reason why I said that is because if he can start out hitting you and you two were only married for a month, that's a sign right there and a serious sign too," Mom said.

I took a deep breath because I knew I had to tell Mom everything about my encounter with Shonda and tell her what she told me. "Mom, when I was at the salon, this young lady came in and sat beside me in the waiting area. Her name is Shonda and she's Steven's ex-girlfriend and the mother of his child.

Shonda told me some things about Steven. She told me that Steven is extremely abusive, along with him being bipolar and schizophrenic. She told me one minute he could be the kindest person and all of a sudden he would just snap on you. At first I told Shonda I didn't believe her and she told me if I get home after Steven gets off from work, then I'll see for myself.

At first I thought Shonda was lying and that she was only saying those things to break us up but Mom, the way this young lady was shaking and trembling, as if she was afraid that Steven would walk in the salon any minute, I knew she was telling me the truth. She told me how she saw his medication on the counter one night and when she Googled it to see what kind of medication he was taking, is when she realized what he had.

She found out it was to treat bipolar and schizophrenic patients. Shonda told me that Steven tried to kill her when he realized she knew what kind of medication he was taking. Shonda said, she knew it had to be God for the reason she ended up getting out of that apartment alive.

Shonda told me that Steven and her son Stephan are the same way. He has that same mental illness. Stephan has it so bad that's he's in a locked down facility. Shonda said she couldn't handle him and she didn't want her son to end up killing her or himself. That's why Stephan doesn't spend time with Steven on the weekend, is because of his level of functioning. There's just no telling what he will do.

Mom, she also told me where Steven keeps his medication in case I wanted to look for myself to confirm her story. Shonda told me about Steven's grandmother that raised him and if anyone could tell me about Steven, it would definitely be her. She wrote down the lady's address on a piece of paper for me.

After all the fighting the police took Steven in the back of their car. I had to see if that medication was in fact where Shonda said it would be and it was. Mom, Steven is a walking time bomb and he's violent. I'm not going to spend my life walking around on eggshells just to get along with him. That's no way to live and I will not allow my son to live in that kind of chaos either, just for the sake of being married. Calvin's happiness means everything to me as well as my own. I won't let Steven take that away from us. Not now, not ever," I said.

"Good for you baby. No one should jeopardize their own happiness or their children's happiness for anyone. It's not worth it. This will always be you and Calvin's home. You can stay here as long as you want or need to," Mom said. "Thank you Mom. That means a lot to me to know you have my back," I said.

"I always will Tammy. Always remember that," Mom said, getting up and giving me a hug. "You get you some rest and I'll see you in the morning," Mom said. "Goodnight Mom," I said.

I sat in the living room for a few more minutes, just reflecting back on what happened earlier tonight with Steven. That's probably one of the scariest things, is to love someone and see them turn into someone that you don't recognize. As much as I love Steven, I think it's best to let him go his way and I'll go mine.

Chapter 12

Steven's Grandmother

I GOT UP AND TOOK CALVIN to school and headed back home. I didn't want to have to explain the bruise across my face from when Steven hit me last night. This was going to be my first and last time calling out from work, because of Steven's abuse.

Steven must have posted his bail yesterday because he started texting and calling me early this morning, telling me he was sorry and that he loves me and apologizing for how he acted. I simply ignored his text messages and phone calls and then I blocked him. I wasn't going to play these games anymore with him.

I got up and took a shower to prepare myself for today. I wanted to visit Mrs. Lucille so I could talk to her. I need to know what she could tell me about Steven.

I grabbed my keys off the table and headed out to Gable, South Carolina. I thought Manning had some country areas but Gable is definitely out there. I've always heard that you better be careful driving through Gable and Turbeville because of the speed traps.

I pulled up to a white old board house. I knocked on the door and this older lady came to the door. "Hello. May I help you?" the woman asked. "Hello. I'm looking for Mrs. Lucille Gibbons," I said. "Okay, well who's looking for her?" the woman asked. "Her grandson's wife," I said. "Which one of my grandsons did you marry? I have ten grandsons," the woman said.

"I'm married to Steven," I said. "Okay. The crazy one," the woman said, as she burst out laughing. I didn't respond. "Come on in the house child so we can talk and I'll tell you what you want to know," Mrs. Lucille said.

I followed Mrs. Lucille in the house and sat on the couch. Mrs. Lucille's house was absolutely beautiful on the inside. You would've never imagined her house looked like this, compared to how it looked on the outside. "May I offer you some tea?" Mrs. Lucille asked. "No ma'am, I'm fine. I'll stay in the bathroom, while I'm trying to drive back," I said. Mrs. Lucille laughed. "So tell me young lady, what do you want to know about Steven? Is he really crazy and used to do all kinds of crazy things growing up? If that's what you came for, I could've told you that on the phone and you wouldn't have wasted a trip all the way up here.

I swear that boy use to do some crazy stuff growing up. I guess it's not all his fault. My husband's family has a history of mental illness. I didn't know that when I met him and had children by him though.

My husband has two sisters and one brother with those kinds of problems. I had six children, two sons and a daughter who suffered from mental illness. Steven's mother, Anna would've been my oldest child but Steven's father killed her," Mrs. Lucille said. "How did he kill her?" I asked. "He shot her in the head with his shot gun in front of Steven and his brother Tony.

Those two have seen and been through a lot. Tony is a lot worse off than Steven, because he stayed in trouble for robbing and raping people and things. Tony didn't care if he was raping a woman, a man, or as sick as it sounds, someone's dog, pig or anything that had a hole. Tony just wanted it and he didn't care who or what it came from," Mrs. Lucille said.

I just shook my head, hating the visual image that just popped in my head when she said that. "What about Steven?" I asked. "Well Steven was a different kind of crazy. That boy was so freaking smart, until it was crazy and he was so good with his hands. Steven would wake up in the middle of the night around one or two in the morning and clean the entire house. He would have breakfast laid out on top of the stove that he made and dinner for that day as well.

The crazy thing was Steven would get back in bed and would get up in the morning, like he had no idea who made all that food. I don't know if he was afraid he would get into trouble for cooking when everyone was asleep or if he actually didn't remember doing it. We had a black and white dog named "Lucky" and

Lucky was a female dog so she would have about three litters of puppies each year. Steven would sit for hours, watching Lucky nurse her puppies and the evil look he had in his eyes was quite disturbing. One morning we woke up and found Lucky and all the puppies' heads chopped off their bodies. They were all in a circle and Lucky's head was in the middle.

Child, I knew right then that Steven and Tony had to get the hell up out of my house before me and my husband lay down one night, and they find our heads cut off our bodies and cooking in a big pot of soup or something. My husband and I had to send them away so they could get some help because we definitely couldn't keep them around here.

Child, I almost fell over when one of my daughters told me that they heard that Steven got married, my heart went out to the young lady. I guess that young lady is you. Please tell me you don't have any children from him?" Mrs. Lucille asked. "No ma'am. I don't," I said. "Good baby. These days in time you have to be careful who you're marrying and who you're having children by.

Young lady, when Steven got grown, he got himself together and went to college and now he's a doctor. I sure wouldn't let him work or touch my body and Lord watch over the people that's crazy enough to let him work on their bodies. Steven disowned everyone that reminded him of his past growing up. He never comes by to see me or his grandfather. He and his brother Tony don't talk either.

Steven didn't invite any of us to his wedding. I guess he was too afraid of someone telling you what kind of person he is, but who knows what his reason was. But baby, something must have happened for you to be here though? What did he do?" Mrs. Lucille asked.

I took a deep breath and told Mrs. Lucille everything. Mrs. Lucille shook her head as I was talking. "Baby, do you have any children? I know you told me that you and Steven don't have children but do you have any yourself?" Mrs. Lucille asked. "I have a son that I'm raising," I said. "Okay, look if you have any problems with him harassing you, take out a restraining order and then get you a gun. Learn how to shoot that gun because sometimes baby, some people with mental illness, don't know how to accept the word "no," until something tragic happens. You seem like a sweet and loving person and I hate to see something happen to you because you didn't take my advice," Mrs. Lucille said. "You're right Mrs. Lucille and I'm going to do just that today," I said.

"Please do sweetheart. The last thing I want to read about you in the newspaper or see your face on the news, saying what my grandson did to you. Jump on that as soon as possible. Look, even if you have to tell the police lies that he is harassing you and bothering you in order for you to get that restraining order, that's what you need to do. So all that will be in place in case something happens and you have to take the law in your own hands.

The last thing you need is to be is not prepared and need to be prepared. I stood up and hugged Mrs. Lucille and gave her a hug. "It was so nice meeting and talking to you Mrs. Lucille. And please don't ever tell Steven or anyone that I came by talking to you. I don't want it to get back to Steven and he comes around causing my family trouble," I said. "Baby, I will never do that. Trust me, your secret is safe here. I hope this won't be your last time visiting me but if it is, I'll totally understand," Mrs. Lucille said. "Thank you Mrs. Lucille. I really do appreciate that," I said, as she walked me to my car.

As I started driving, I thought about my conversation with Mrs. Lucille and she definitely shed a lot of light on things for me, and I'm going straight down to the police station to get things in place, like the restraining order and getting myself a registered gun. Mrs. Lucille said even if I have to lie to get one put in place, then that's exactly what I'm willing to do.

Chapter 13

A Star

I DECIDED TO STOP BY THE grocery store and get a few things to make dinner for us tonight, instead of Mom always cooking. I told Mom that I would pick Calvin up from school today. Calvin was excited today because he said they were taking them to the YMCA for the kids to go swimming and for them to play basketball, if the kids choose not to swim.

I gave him ten dollars along with a change of clothes and a few towels. I just finished dinner and took it out of the stove and placed it on top of the stove. I looked at my watch and saw it was time for me to pick Calvin up from YMCA.

I sure hope he had a good time and I'm sure he'll have a lot to talk about how his day was. There's a few little boys in the neighborhood for Calvin to play with, but I'm a little afraid to let him go out to play with them. Those little boys are a little rough and Calvin isn't used to all that. I think I'm going to sign him up for Karate classes pretty soon so he will learn how to defend himself if he needs to, like how my Dad did for me.

As I drove through the light, I thought about Shemika and wondered how she's doing. I still haven't heard anything from her, other than that video message she sent to me a few years ago, telling me she needed to get herself together and apologizing for just leaving and dropping Calvin off on me but now I look at it as a blessing.

At first I was hurt that she would do me like that, to have me watch her son, only to dump him off on me and never call or returned. I had to alter my entire life around what she did, but I couldn't have done any of this without my mother's help. My mother was there one hundred percent and she promised me that I wouldn't have to do any of it by myself and I haven't. My mother is the real MVP in my life.

I pulled up to the YMCA and walked inside. "Hello. I'm here to pick up my son, Calvin Martin," I said. "Okay. I think he is the only student left. His teacher just came up front, looking for you. Let me call her upfront on the intercom. "Mrs. Conyers, Calvin's mother is here to pick him up," the woman said.

I was a little embarrassed that all the other childrens' parents had already picked up their child and I was the last one getting here. "Ms. Evette Conyers walked upfront with Calvin and some tall brown-skinned man. "Who is this?" I said to myself, as they both approached me with Calvin.

"Hey Tamara, it's nice to see you again," Evette said, as she reached out to hug me. Evette and I are classmates. She and I have always been cool and in fact she came to my wedding. "Hey Evette. Is there something going on?" I asked, wondering why this man was walking with her and Calvin. "No, not at all. This is Coach Dammon White and he's one of the little league basketball coaches here at the YMCA. He wanted to talk to you about Calvin.

I'll let you both talk, and I can head on out. "Glad you had a good time today Calvin and Tamara, you enjoy your day," Evette said, as she walked off.

"Hey Mom," Calvin said, giving me a hug. "Hey son." I said, returning his hug. "Hello Mr. White, nice to meet you," I said. "Please call me Dammon, and nice to meet you as well. I'm not going to take up much of your time but I had about ten boys out of Calvin's class in the gym with me playing basketball. We let the goals down for their height so they could be able to shoot the ball in and Lord, Calvin was killing everyone.

Your son is a natural basketball player. It's almost like he was born with a basketball in his hands. Would you be interested in letting Calvin work with me at the YMCA? I coach a little league basketball team and I would be honored to have Calvin play for us. We practice every day about an hour and then we normally have a game on Wednesdays and Thursdays and sometimes Saturdays. I would really like it if you would let me work with him and let him be on my team.

I'll pick him up from school and bring him here. I can even drop him off back home or you and your husband could come pick him up from here, if you would like? I don't want to inconvenience either one of you," Dammon said. "Well, my husband and I are no longer together, so he won't be a problem and we're getting a divorce, so he won't be dropping him off anywhere. I'm still on defense about all this though. Calvin should be spending his time doing his homework and playing like a normal kid," I said.

I don't want to put it in his head, that all to life is playing sports and not getting a good education," I said. "Well, Mrs. Williams," Dammon called my married last name. Just the sound of that name made chills go up my spine and not in a good way. "Please Dammon, just call me Tamara," I said. "Okay. Tamara, I won't let Calvin's grades start slipping and him playing basketball can really possibly get him into a good college," Dammon said.

"Well him being smart is going to get him into a good college as well. I don't want Calvin thinking that people are going to just give him a free pass in life because he can dribble a basketball good or throw a football or get a touchdown here and there. His education has to come first," I said.

"Well, I totally understand everything you're saying but we're not talking about him playing in the NBA right now, he's just playing with the little league basketball team and that's it," Dammon said, laughing.

I looked at Calvin and he really looked like he wanted to play and I didn't want to feel and look like the big bad mom, that stopped my son from playing and doing what he wanted to do. "Look, if my son's grades or his homework starts slipping for one reason, it's going to be his behind and yours as well. Do you hear me?" I said. "Yes ma'am I do," Dammon replied.

"Calvin, would you like to play basketball for the YMCA for little league?" I asked. "Yes Mom. I really would," Calvin said, with desperation in his eyes. "Okay, I'll let you do it but those grades better not start slipping or you're not doing your homework," I said. "Okay Mom," Calvin said.

"Mom, can I get a soda from the soda machine?" Calvin asked. "Sure, but don't drink it until we have dinner," I said, giving him a don't try me kind of look, and handing him three dollars.

Calvin walked over to the soda machine. "Dammon, is he really that good?" I asked. "Tamara, I think you have a real basketball star on your hands. Calvin just needs to learn a little basketball discipline and learn how to dribble a little but with some techniques and I think we might be looking at the next Michael Jordan," Dammon said. I just smiled at the confidence Dammon had in Calvin. I hope this will be something he would really be interested in.

Chapter 14

Mr. Crazy

I CLOCKED IN AT WORK AND went around to do my rounds. Mrs. Ollie Mae was sitting on the bed watching TV. "Good morning, Mrs. Ollie Mae. How are you?" I asked, giving her a hug. "I'm doing good now that my favorite pretty black nurse is here," Mrs. Ollie Mae said, as she hugged me.

I smiled at Mrs. Ollie Mae's comment because ever since I became an RN here, she's been calling me that. She told me all the time how proud she is of me that I went on to finish school to become a nurse, instead of stopping at just being a CNA. She told me I deserve to be a RN since I have a son to support.

If no one else at work acts like they love me, it doesn't matter because I know Mrs. Ollie Mae does. "Have you taken your morning shower yet?" I asked. "No I haven't. The young lady was going to help me take one before she got off but I told her no thank you, that I was waiting on you," Mrs. Ollie Mae said. "What did she say when you said that?" I asked. "Nothing. She just rolled her eyes and then she said, I swear you love that old Tamara, don't you?" Mrs. Ollie Mae said.

I laughed at her response because I knew Mrs. Ollie Mae was going to tell me exactly what she told her. "Tammy, I told her I sure do and then she left. I guess she didn't like that response," Mrs. Ollie Mae said.

"I missed you yesterday. Why didn't you come to work?" Mrs. Ollie Mae asked. "Oh, I had some business to take care of," I said. Mrs. Ollie Mae put her hand on my shoulder and pulled her face closer towards me and shook her head.

"You know makeup is a wonderful thing isn't it? It can hide things like scars and bruises that we don't want people to see. The only thing about makeup is, you have to eventually wash it off and that same scar or hurtful bruise is still there. The bad thing is, you remember who put it there and why. So why did your husband do that?" Mrs. Ollie Mae asked.

I swear, this old woman is so wise and can see through anything and definitely straight through me. "That's why you didn't come to work yesterday, because you wanted your face to heal some and I'm sure it has healed some since the day it happened.

The only thing is people like me that know and love you, know something is up, especially when a certain beautiful young lady, just started wearing makeup, that never wore it before. Now are you going to tell me why he did that, especially since you two haven't been married long at all?" Mrs. Ollie Mae asked.

I didn't want to tell this woman my personal business but she already saw it and pretty much cracked the case wide open in the first place, so I might as well tell her the truth. "Yes Mrs. Ollie Mae, my husband did this to me," I said, as I told her all that happened.

Mrs. Ollie Mae grabbed my hand the entire time I was talking to her. "That fool was trying to kill me. I had to fight back with everything I had in me and believe me, a sister had to fight like hell to survive. I knew I couldn't leave my son without his mother and I did everything to make sure I was going to watch him grow up.

I called the police and they came and arrested Steven. Steven must have posted bail because he was out the next day and begging me to give him another chance," I said.

Mrs. Ollie Mae shook her head. "Lord girl, you're married to Mr. Crazy. You two haven't even been married for two months yet and he's already putting his hands on you. Baby, imagine if you two were married for years, what you probably would have to endure? Tammy, I know you never expected your new marriage to end like this but trust me, it's ended.

You don't ever want to question your husband's intention in your marriage, whether or not it was an accident or did I bring this on myself? Could I have communicated better to him, that I was getting my hair done? Tammy, no woman should ever feel that they need to walk on eggshells, afraid of upsetting their husband.

You're married to a crazy man that seems unstable and has an insecure problem of feeling abandoned from you and dealt with abandonment many times before," Mrs. Ollie Mae said.

"Mrs. Ollie Mae, Steven witnessed his father shot and kill his mother in the head and right in front of Steven and his brother. That's a lot for someone to endure as a child, especially already experiencing mental illness issues too. I don't want to lay beside Steven and not wake up again because he murdered me in my sleep.

I can't live like that, Mrs. Ollie Mae. I won't live like that," I said. "Good baby. You don't deserve to live like that. I sure hope you got a restraining order on his behind because something tells me that Mr. Crazy isn't going to give up so easily," Mrs. Ollie Mae said. "You're right. I don't think he will as well," I replied. "Then you better get you a gun for protection and carry that gun at all times. Someone like your crazy husband, you can never be too careful with a situation like that," Mrs. Ollie Mae replied. "I totally agree," I said, helping Mrs. Ollie Mae put on her shoes.

Chapter 15

Bring My Son Home

I JUST GOT IN MY CAR after getting off from work. I leaned my head back in my car, feeling kind of weird. I had a strange feeling all day, like I felt something was going to happen and I couldn't shake it.

I pulled out of the parking lot as my cell phone started ringing. I looked at my phone and saw it was Mom calling. "Hey Mom. How are you?" I asked. "Baby, it's Calvin." Mom said, as I could tell something was definitely wrong. My heart nearly stopped and I quickly slammed on brakes, on the side of the street. "Mom, what's wrong with my baby?" I asked. "Tammy, he's not here. I'm here at the school to pick him up and the receptionist said he went with his stepfather Mr. Steven Williams. Steven signed Calvin out," Mom said.

I suddenly got sick to my stomach and I couldn't breathe. "Baby, are you still here? Did you hear what I said?" Mom asked. I couldn't speak. I was having an anxiety attack. I quickly grabbed the paper bag that was in my glove compartment and started breathing into it slowly. "Breathe baby, breathe," Mom said. I guess Mom knew what was going on with me.

I started taking my time to inhale and exhale slowly, to catch my breath. "Keep breathing sweetie, you're doing so good," Mom said, giving me words of encouragement.

I did my breathing techniques that I learned as a child and was able to get through my panic anxiety attack. I haven't had one of those since I was about twelve.

"Mom, tell me what happened?" I asked. "Well I went to pick Calvin up from school and the receptionist gave me a puzzled look and told me that Calvin just left with his stepfather about an hour ago." "Mom, I forgot to remove Steven's name from the emergency contact list for early dismissal or in case he was to get sick. How could I have forgotten to do that! What should I do? Should I call the police?" I asked.

"Why don't you call Steven first and tell him if Calvin isn't returned back home in the next thirty minutes, you're going to call the police," Mom said. "Okay. I'll do that Mom, because if I call the police, they will take his behind straight to jail because my restraining order covers our family, and fifty feet from being near us. I just forgot to inform the school of the change though. I'll do that as soon as I have Calvin back," I said.

"Tammy, call Steven now because maybe he has no intentions of hurting Calvin and he just wanted to get your attention," Mom said. "Okay. I'm going to call that fool and tell him he has thirty minutes to have my son back home or I'm calling the police," I said. "Okay baby. Call me back," Mom said.

I hung up the phone with Mom and then unblocked Steven's number. Steven answered the phone. "Hello," Steven answered the phone all calmly, as if he had no idea why I'm calling him in the first place. "Where is my son!" I yelled. "He is with me. I bought him some school clothes and took him out to the mall to get some ice cream. We're on our way back to your house now," Steven replied. "Oh, now you want to spend time with him? You didn't want to be bothered when we all were living together right?" I asked. Steven paused for a few seconds, before he said anything else. I guess he thought about what I just said to him.

"I've changed Tamara, and if you give me another chance, I can show you that," Steven said. I wanted to curse Steven out so badly but I had to hold my tongue at least until I get Calvin back home, where he belongs. "Steven you have exactly thirty minutes to get my son back home before I call the police. Do you understand?" I said, hanging up the phone.

I turned my emergency lights on and went flying home. I tried my best to not hit cars or get stopped by the police but I didn't care. All I wanted was to see my son and hold him in my arms. I want to grab Calvin and squeeze him so tightly and never let him go.

It's amazing how motherhood has changed me and made me into a different person, now that I have Calvin. If anyone would tell me that I would be a mother at age twenty-one, I wouldn't believe them, especially after I was told I would never be able to bear children. At first I was devastated and I think I cried for about a month straight, but God allowed one of my best friends to have a child and blessed me with him, since she wasn't ready to be a parent yet.

I guess it might be a blessing in disguise that I couldn't have children, especially since I found out about Steven's anger issues, along with his mental illness and history of the gene. I wouldn't want to bring a child in the world like that and eventually end up putting my child in a lockdown facility like Shonda had to do with Stephan. I'm praying for her and Stephan every day for healing over his mind and body. That has to be a horrible thing to see your child going through that and knowing there's nothing you can do to help him.

I pulled up in the driveway beside Mom's car and ran in the house. I'm so glad that I took Mrs. Lucille's advice and got a gun to defend and protect myself and my family.

I grabbed my gun out of the lockbox in the top of my closet and sat on the porch, waiting for Steven to bring my baby back home. Mom came to the door and saw the gun sitting in my lap. "Lord child, what in the world are you going to do with that gun, Tammy?" Mom asked. "Whatever means necessary!" I said.

"Baby, don't do anything you might regret," Mom said. "Mom, I'm going to do whatever I have to do to protect my family. I'm going to let Steven know that I'm not going to live in fear and neither will you or Calvin.

Mom kept trying to reason with me, when Steven finally pulled up in the yard. He got out of the car carrying bags in his hands as well as Calvin. I stood up and put the gun down in the chair and put a towel on top of it so Calvin couldn't see it. Steven walked Calvin up to the porch. "Hey Mommy," Calvin said, smiling, as I grabbed and hugged him tightly, feeling the tears coming down my face. It felt good to hold my son in my arms. This was a feeling that I never wanted to forget.

"Mom, look what Steve bought me. He bought me a lot of clothes and new shoes. Mom, why are you crying?" Calvin asked, as he noticed my tears. "Look, go in the house with your grandma and put your new things on your bed so you can show them to me when I come inside," I said. "Okay Mommy," Calvin said. "Here Calvin, can you grab these two bags too?" Steven asked. "I'll grab them," Mom said, walking off the porch to take the bags from Steven. "How you doing Mrs. Carolyn?" Steven asked.

"I'm doing well Steven. How are you?" Mom asked, taking the bags from Steven. "I'm doing good," Steven said. Mom took Calvin inside and closed the front door.

I grabbed my gun out of the chair and held it in my hand. "Whoa Tamara. What are you doing?" Steven asked, backing up, holding up his hands. "Look, I'm only going to say this one time and one time only. You are not welcome here, around me or my family. The restraining order states that you can't be within fifty feet from us at all times.

Steven, you can't come anywhere near my job or my house again. Calvin is off limits to you and I totally forgot to remove your name from the emergency contact or as one of the people to pick him up from school, but I will do that first thing in the morning. Our life together is over with. The divorce papers will be in the mail by next week. Please sign the papers and send them back to my lawyer so we can move on with our lives," I said.

Steven stood there just looking at me and then dried the tears that fell down his face. "I'm so sorry that I hurt you, my beautiful wife. Tamara, I need help and I'm getting help for my anger. I know it doesn't matter what I say, beg or plead with you, you're not going to give me another chance. I can't say that I blame you because I could only imagine what I must have looked like to you when I acted the way I did that night.

All I can say is I'm so sorry for hurting you but I don't want a divorce, but I know you do. When the divorce papers come in the mail, I'll sign them and put them back in the mail. You won't have any problems out of me. This was a misunderstanding today.

I tried calling you on your cell but I couldn't get through to you. I texted you but I got a "not available" reply back so I guess you have me blocked, so I used my emergency hospital phone and called and texted you. I even left a voicemail as well. I also texted and called your mom and left her a voicemail too, I just wanted to see Calvin and get him some stuff, that's all. I didn't mean any harm.

I'll leave and I won't bother you, Calvin, or your mother again. Tamara, I'm really sorry and I hope you can one day forgive me and I'll never stop loving you. Good-bye for now," Steven said, as he walked to his car and got inside. I watched Steven as he drove off, hopefully for the last time. I believe that he's actually sorry for his actions that night but what's done is done and we can't change that now. Steven said he'll always love me and I believe him because I'll always love him, we just can't be together anymore.

Chapter 16

Everything Will Work Out

I WAS PRETTY MUCH OUT OF it today, still upset about what Steven did yesterday. How in the world did he just think it was okay to take my son like that, without saying a word to me? I'm sure he saw on the restraining order that he has to stay fifty feet away from me and my family.

The shocking thing is that Steven didn't want to spend time with Calvin when we were living there in the house with him and now he wants to. He'd rather stay locked up in our bedroom and wouldn't even talk to him.

I didn't go in Mrs. Ollie Mae's room this morning, because I knew if she saw me, she would know something was wrong. I went to everyone's room except hers to do my rounds and as I was coming back up front, she jumped out of her room, just when I was walking by, almost scaring me to death.

"So you're avoiding me huh?" Mrs. Ollie Mae asked. "No ma'am, I'm not," I said. "Tammy, stop lying and get in here," Mrs. Ollie Mae said. I swear this lady can read me like a freaking book.

I walked in her room and closed the door behind me. "Good morning Mrs. Ollie Mae. How are you?" I asked. "Don't you good morning me. What is wrong with you and why are you avoiding me?" Mrs. Ollie asked. "I'm not avoiding you," I said, looking down. "Oh Lord. What did that crazy husband of yours do this time?" Mrs. Ollie Mae asked.

I shook my head at her comment. "He didn't do anything," I said. "Okay if you don't want to talk about it, then that's fine but don't tell me he didn't do anything because I know better and I can see it all over your face," Mrs. Ollie Mae said.

I helped Mrs. Ollie Mae take off her gown so I could help her into the shower. I decided to open up to her. Maybe I'll feel better if I do. "Mrs. Ollie Mae, Steven took my son without my permission yesterday from school. He took him school shopping and then took him out to eat and got him ice cream. Steven only did it to mess with me because he knew I have a restraining order that covers me and my entire family. He knows he can't come within fifty feet of us, and he pulled that stunt.

When my mother called me yesterday afternoon and told me that Calvin wasn't at school and they released him to my husband, I saw red. I wanted to beat that fool down with my bare hands. I can handle him coming for me but don't put my son in our mess. What he and I are going through, doesn't have anything to do with Calvin," I said.

"So let me get this straight? Your husband picked your child up from school, without your permission and took him school shopping and you have a restraining order against him, that includes your entire family?" Mrs. Ollie Mae asked. "Yes, that's correct. I know it sounds crazy doesn't it?" I said. "It sure does. Your husband's name is Steven right? Are you planning on changing your last name back to Martin?" Mrs. Ollie Mae asked. "Yes I am. I don't like my last name being Williams. I don't want anything that belongs to my husband," I said.

Mrs. Ollie Mae shook her head. "I wonder why your husband is so crazy?" Mrs. Ollie Mae asked. "Well Steven's grandmother told me that mental illness runs in their family on Steven's grandfather's side. Steven's grandmother told me that Tony and Steven used to do some strange things growing up as kids, and then his father shot and killed his mother in front of Steven and his brother.

I'm sure that has a lot to do with his mental state right now. I know I can't walk around in fear of being married to someone like Steven, not knowing who or what I'm going to lay down with that night or who I'm going to wake up to that morning. Hell, dealing with him, I don't know if I'll even wake up in the morning if he doesn't kill me in my sleep. That's no way for a person to live," I said.

I could tell my story deeply hurt Mrs. Ollie Mae, because she had tears in her eyes. I think she knew what I went through because something tells me that she might have gone through something similar as well. Now was my time to ask her about her past. She shouldn't mind sharing with me since she stayed up in my business all the time.

"Mrs. Ollie Mae, how was your husband? Was he a good man?" I asked. "Baby, which one? You know I've been married three times. My first husband which was my children's father was a good man until he died but my second husband wasn't so good. And you know my third husband was a pastor of First Clarendon. My second husband is the one I had so many problems with and nearly killed myself.

Tammy, my husband barely worked and he expected me to pay all the bills. My husband and I had no children together but I had two children from my first marriage.

It's hard being a parent these days but what's even harder is when you think you married a good man, only to realize what you married is a monster. I remember my children's teachers would call me at work, telling me that Donna and Richie were fighting and got suspended from school.

Tammy, my children's teachers would tell me how they would be talking back and very disruptive in class. I asked my children what was going on with them because that wasn't like them to be acting like that. Neither one of my children would talk to me or tell me anything. I asked them if anything was wrong or was there something they needed to tell me and they would always shake their heads and tell me "no."

One day I left them home on a Saturday morning to go grocery shopping, while they were in bed. I told my husband where I was going but I didn't wake up the kids. What I did was I went to the park and waited about forty-five minutes and then I came back home.

Tammy, I couldn't shake the feeling that something was going on in my house and I needed to know. So I parked the car by my mailbox and sneaked inside my house. I went to my bedroom first and my husband was out of bed. I went to the bathroom, kitchen and even back to the living room but my husband wasn't in any of those rooms.

I then tiptoed to my son's Richie's room and my husband was molesting both my children on the bed. He's been doing that for years under my nose and I didn't even know about it. I ran straight to my kitchen and grabbed a butcher knife and ran back in my son's room, like a maniac.

I started swinging the knife back and forth and stabbed my husband in the arm. I saw my son's wooden baseball bat in the corner of his room and started beating the hell out of my husband, screaming "You are my husband and you're their stepfather! You're supposed to love and protect them! You're not supposed to be doing this sick and perverted acts that you're doing to them!"

Tammy, when I finally got off him, I told him he had exactly ten minutes to get whatever clothes he could get out of my house because whatever was left, I was burning up everything else. Two days later, they found him on the side of the road dead and a knife was in his chest.

No one ever found out what happened to my husband and to be honest, I didn't care if he was murdered or not. I was just glad to know he wasn't going to ever hurt my children again and that he was out of my life for good.

A parent, especially a mother would move heaven and earth to protect their children and try to shield them from getting hurt like picking out their friends, from the ones they need to stay away from or that person that they're dating, knowing they're not going to treat them right. But Tammy, at some point we have to let them make their own mistakes and their own decisions. We can't choose everything for them," Mrs. Ollie Mae said.

"I'm so sorry that happened to you and your children, Mrs. Ollie Mae. No child should have to go through that," I said. "You're right, but Tammy to be honest I think my children would've kept that from me until they died if I didn't find out about it myself. God had a reason to let me go to the park and wait like that, because there was something at my house that I had to see and I'm glad that I trusted what God and my instinct was telling me. Trust me Tammy, everything is going to be alright," Mrs. Ollie Mae said, and I believe that it definitely will.

Chapter 17

A Phone Call

MOM MADE DINNER TONIGHT AND all three of us were sitting in the living room watching Wheel of Fortune. Calvin told us how well he was doing at the YMCA. His first game is this Saturday. I told Calvin his grandmother and I would be there. He asked if I could invite Ms. Sarah and Abbigail to come. I told him I'll definitely ask but if they didn't come then that wasn't up to me. Calvin said he understood.

I thought about Mrs. Ollie Mae and my conversation earlier and I told Calvin if anyone touched him or tried to make him do something he doesn't like to, please let me or an adult know as soon as possible but whoever he tells it to, he still needs to make sure he tells me as well.

I used Calvin's teddy bear that Mom bought him when he was three years old, to show him the difference between a good touch and a bad touch. Calvin told me he understood, which I knew he did because he's very smart and picks up on things very easily.

I jumped when I heard someone knocking on the front door. "Mom, are you expecting anyone?" I asked. "No baby. Are you?" Mom asked. "No ma'am," I said, going to the door. "Who is it?" I asked. "Ma'am it's the police, could we speak to Mrs. Tamara Martin Williams? We have some important questions to ask her," the officer said.

I opened the door and turned on the porch light and stepped on the front porch with them. There were two officers, a male and a female. "Hello ma'am. I'm Officer Shelby and this is Officer Lawson, the male officer said, pointing to the female officer. "What is this about?" I asked, ready for them to get to the point of why they were here.

"Ma'am, are you related to Mr. Steven Williams?" Officer Shelby asked. "Yes, that's my husband but soon to be ex-husband," I said. "Ma'am, your husband was attacked today around six-forty this afternoon," the police said. "Oh my God. Is he okay?" I asked. "Ma'am he's alive but seriously hurt. He probably has a long road to recovery though," Officer Lawson said.

"Ma'am, your husband was attacked leaving work in the hospital parking lot. Three guys jumped him and started beating him with aluminum baseball bats. They broke both of his legs and one of his arms. He has a concussion as well. The last time we checked, he hasn't regained consciousness yet.

We know you two are in the process of filing for a divorce and that you took out a restraining order out on him. Why is that?" Officer Lawson asked. "Well if you know all that, then why don't you know why I took out a restraining order out on him?" I asked, rolling my eyes. Officer Shelby and Officer Lawson, had a blank look on their faces. Let me answer these people's questions so I can get them away from our house. "My husband is a violent man and he suffers from mental illness. One particular night he tried killing me, because I didn't come home until much later," I said.

"Ma'am, did you hire anyone to set up your husband or to beat him up? I guess to pay him back for what he did to you," Officer Shelby asked. "Of course not. I would never do anything like that," I said. "Well do you know if your husband has any enemies? I mean do you know anyone that would want him dead?" Officer Shelby asked.

"Sir, my husband could be a hothead at times. You know the kind that barks all day but when you raise up to him, he sometimes backs down, unless he's fussing with a woman or something," I said. "Okay, well can you tell us where were you around six-thirty and six-forty-five?" Officer Shelby asked. "I was right here with my mother and my son and if you don't mind, I would like to get back to them now," I said.

"Certainly ma'am, we're sorry for disturbing you and your family this evening," Officer Lawson said, as they walked off the porch. "Look, is my husband here at Manning hospital or Sumter?" I asked. "He's at the hospital here in Manning," Officer Lawson said, as they walked back to their patrol car.

I came back in the house and sat down on the couch. I told Mom and Calvin what happened and they just couldn't believe it, but then again Mom said all that meanness finally caught up with Steven and someone showed him he's not as tough as he thinks he is. I told Mom I totally agree. A giant can be so much bigger and taller than you but they can fall down just as anyone else can.

I just got to work and did all my rounds. I saved Mrs. Ollie Mae for the last person on my list to do my rounds with since she likes for me and only me, to give her a shower. "Good morning Mrs. Ollie Mae. Are you ready for your shower?" I asked, as I reached over and gave her a hug. "I sure am," Mrs. Ollie Mae said.

I helped Mrs. Ollie Mae in the bathroom to help her take off her clothes. I adjusted the water for her, as she sat on the shower chair. "So how's that husband of yours? Is he keeping his hands to himself?" Mrs. Ollie Mae asked, with a wicked smile on her face. "Mrs. Ollie Mae, you know we aren't together anymore. He lives at his house and I live with my mom and Calvin," I said. "Yes, I remember you telling me that, but it should be hard for him to bother you or take little Calvin, without your permission since he's in the hospital right?" Mrs. Ollie Mae said.

"Mrs. Ollie Mae, how do you know my husband is in the hospital? I never told anyone that, especially since I just found out last night," I said. "Because I made a phone call and had my nephew put a little crew together and they took care of business for me. Tammy, I don't like to see anyone being bullied, especially by someone that claims to love them. I'm sure after your husband gets out of the hospital, he'll leave you and your family alone and never bother you again. Let's just say I made sure of that," Mrs. Ollie Mae said.

At first I thought Mrs. Ollie Mae was lying but how in the world did she know he was in the hospital? I didn't tell her and I definitely didn't tell any of these snakes I work with. Could she possibly had set all this up like she said? I don't believe she would do something like that.

"You don't think I had anything to do with what happened to your husband do you? You think a little old woman like me couldn't do anything in a place like this?" Mrs. Ollie Mae asked. "Yes, that's right," I said. "Tammy, go get me my phone out my nightstand, and bring it here," Mrs. Ollie Mae said.

I walked in Mrs. Ollie Mae's room and brought her cell phone. She put her fingerprint in and went to her photo galleries and handed the phone to me. I looked at the picture she showed me, and I almost brought up my breakfast from earlier. The picture showed Steven, lying in the hospital parking lot, in a puddle of blood, and someone showing the peace sign with their two fingers. I couldn't believe what I was seeing. This sweet, little old lady is a little gangster.

"Mrs. Ollie Mae, I didn't ask you to do that. I'm not trying to get in trouble for nothing you had your family do," I said. "Tammy, calm down. You didn't have anything to do with that and no you didn't ask me to take care of it for you but I did.

I consider you like family to me and in my family, we take care of our own. I see you all the time. I see you more than I see my own two children and they live no more than twenty minutes from this nursing home.

I'm from a big family that don't mind getting their hands dirty a little. I protect my family and family doesn't always have to be blood related. It's just people that care and love each other. So give me a hug, and never breathe a word about this to anyone and say thank you," Mrs. Ollie Mae said. "Thank you Mrs. Ollie Mae, and I think it's best for us to delete this picture out of your phone just so the police can't ever find it," I said.

"I think that will be a great idea," Mrs. Ollie Mae said. As I deleted the picture, I couldn't help from smiling at Mrs. Ollie Mae. I didn't particularly care for how she took care of my little issue with Steven but I guess the bottom line is, she took care of it and I'm sure he's never coming around or bothering us again, but then again I don't know.

Steven is like a cockroach, no matter how much you don't want them around, he'll find a way to just pop right back up, so I guess I'll see when that's going to be.

Chapter 18

Mama

MOM AND I WENT TO Calvin's basketball game at school. Lord, the boy scored twenty points in the first quarter. I'm so glad I let Dammon talk me into letting Calvin play basketball at the YMCA, when he was younger. The boy is in the seventh grade and in all the local newspapers, with how well he's doing. I'm so proud of him.

I told Calvin the minute his grades started slipping, is the day he's getting off the team. Calvin, is still on the "A" honor roll and doing very well. I'm so happy to see that. My house phone is ringing off the hook with all these little girls calling for him.

Calvin always said he didn't have time for any girlfriends because his goals were to make it in the NBA so he could buy me and his grandmother a big house and we could stop working. I joked and told Calvin I didn't need three mansions, just one would be enough. Calvin laughed as though he thought that was the funniest thing.

Mom and I told Calvin that pretty soon he'll be dunking all over people left and right, when he gets a little taller. Calvin said he can't wait until he can start doing that. Dammon told Calvin that it's not every day that someone gets twenty points in the first half and another twenty points in the second half. Dammon told Calvin that he really came to play tonight. Calvin laughed and said he certainly did.

I grabbed two pizzas for dinner because I know after leaving his game, I wasn't about to cook anything. We all sat down in the living room and Calvin went to his bedroom. Mom looked a little tired, like she just wanted to rest. Mom took a little nap in the recliner.

I started playing Candy Crush on my phone to occupy some of my time. Before I knew it, I fell asleep on the couch. I jumped when I realized I was asleep. It was eleven-thirty. Mom was still asleep on the recliner, which isn't like her to not be in bed by now.

I got up and got ready to go to bed. "Mom, you ready to go to bed too?" I asked. "Mom, it's time to go to bed," I said, a little louder. Mom didn't wake up. I got up and came closer to her to wake her up but when I grabbed Mom's hand, she was ice cold and her hand dropped down, lifeless.

I grabbed Mom's wrist to check her pulse but there wasn't one. I leaned over and kissed Mom on her forehead. It just hit me that my mother was dead. I went and knocked on Calvin's door. "Come in," Calvin said, sounding like he was half asleep.

I walked up to Calvin, as he sat up in bed. "Calvin, get up so you can tell your grandmother good-bye," I said. "Good-bye? Mom, where is Grandma going at this time of night?" Calvin asked, while rubbing his eyes and standing up. "Let's see," I said.

Calvin walked towards his grandmother in the living room and grabbed her hand. He felt the coldness and then he looked up at me. "Mom, is Grandma dead?" Calvin asked. "Yes baby. Grandma is gone," I said. Calvin sat down on the floor beside Mom's lap as he took her hand and put it against his face and he yelled out.

The way my son yelled out in pain and hurt, it broke my heart. "Grandma, why did you have to leave me now? You were supposed to be there when I get drafted into the NBA. It was going to be you and Mama right there, just like you two have been there the entire time. I'm going to miss you Grandma and I love you so much. I can't imagine not waking up and seeing your beautiful face, making breakfast and laughing at something silly I said. I will always love you," Calvin said, as he stood up and hugged his grandmother and kissed her on the cheek.

I went over to the phone and called 911 and told them what happened and gave them our address and the gentleman told me the police and the coroner were on their way. I guess the police had to make sure that there was no foul play involved.

I walked over to Mom and I'm so glad that I had a few minutes to spend with Mom before the police and coroner got her. I needed this moment with her to have a proper good-bye. "Mom, thank you so much for life that you gave me. You were my mother and my best friend and you taught me so much. You taught me how to be respectful and to always carry myself as a lady and woman of God.

Thank you so much for showing me an example of a virtuous woman. You showed me how to love and you made me feel loved every single day. You shared your caring heart with me and Calvin. You may not have been able to give me all the finer things in life but you did your best and I appreciate that.

Mom, if I could have picked anyone to be my mother, I definitely would've picked you each and every day. This is going to be one of the hardest things I'll probably ever have to do in my life, is to live without you being here. Mom, I'm going to miss you so, so, much but I know you have to move on from your earthly home, just continue to watch over Calvin and me and watch over our home," I said, as I leaned over and kissed Mom on the cheek and hugged her for the last time.

I heard the police siren as I went to open the door, to let them in as well as the coroner in. Calvin held on to his grandmother's leg, still laying his head on her lap. "Please don't take my grandma away. "Please don't take her away from us. Grandma, we still need you. We still need you," Calvin, cried. I helped Calvin up and held him in my arms. "Baby, it's okay to let Mom go. She's lived her life and she had a great life. Now all we have to do is let Mama rest. Mom gave me the key of showing me how to be a good mother and she's able to go home, knowing I'm good now. I think she is pleased with that."

I took Calvin aside so the coroner and his men could do what they had to do. When the men opened the body bag and placed Mom's body inside, I nearly lost it. Reality just hit me that Mama was really gone and she wasn't coming back. As they rolled Mom's body out of the house, I knew I had to be strong for Calvin because we're going to have to get through this together.

Chapter 19

The Set-Up

IT'S BEEN TWO WEEKS SINCE we buried Mom and Lord she's definitely missed. I can still smell her in the house. Mom left me the house, her car and a nice insurance policy for me and for Calvin. She definitely wants Calvin to go to college so the money she left him, he would definitely be able to go with that. Mom wanted us to be taken care of.

Here I am, a single, divorced mother and I still miss and need my mother. I find myself crying every moment, still grieving for her. The funeral service was extremely packed. Mom was only fifty-seven years old, and it seems too young to have passed away from a heart attack, especially with how active Mom was. Mom's job gave me her 401k and the insurance policy she had at work as well.

I know thinking about dying can be crazy and scary, but to think about just going to sleep and never waking up, sounds more peaceful to leave this world to me.

I just got to work, after being away for two weeks. My director Pam told me to take as long as I needed to come back to work. Pam said all the residents have been asking about me and especially Mrs. Ollie Mae. My director said that Mrs. Ollie Mae was in the hospital for about a week due to having pneumonia. She told me you could hear the rattling in her chest. The doctors told them to have her sit up most of the day. They didn't want her lungs to get back infected and cause her to get pneumonia again.

I walked in to do my rounds and knocked on Mrs. Ollie Mae's door and walked inside. Mrs. Ollie Mae was sitting in her recliner, reading the Bible. "Good morning. How are you Mrs. Ollie Mae?" I asked. "I'm better now baby, after seeing your beautiful face," Mrs. Ollie Mae said, as she reached out her arms to hug me. I returned her hug and tried all I could to muster up a smile. "Are you ready for your shower?" I asked. "Not right now," Mrs. Ollie Mae said.

I just nodded my head at her response. After all these years since I've worked here, Mrs. Ollie Mae has never told me that before. She was always ready. I sat beside her on her bed. "Tammy, first of all, I want to offer my condolences for the loss of your mother. By listening to you talk about her, I could tell you two were very close.

By listening to you talk about your mother, made me realize just how much I miss my own children that never come by to see me. Tammy, my daughter Donna lives only twenty or twenty-five minutes away and I see her one time every two years or so. My son Richie never comes by and he's only ten or fifteen minutes away from this nursing home but he always finds a way to call around Christmas or his birthday for his gift.

When Christmas comes around they don't even say Merry Christmas Mom, they just ask about gifts for their kids or for themselves. Tammy, I don't even hear from them on Mother's Day or my birthday. You know, you're more of a daughter to me than they ever have been.

Sometimes, I sit here and I get so lonely and baby, it hurts so bad to know I have two children that live in the same town and I never see them. My grandson Lane is the only one that comes and sees me. Lane is married and has two children but he tries to come visit at least every other Saturday or Sunday.

Tammy, I don't think I have much longer here on earth and it will be nice to at least see them all before I die," Mrs. Ollie Mae said. I had tears in my eyes listening to Mrs. Ollie Mae's story because Lord knows how much I loved my mom and I would've never done her like that. It was time for me to give this woman some peace and put a smile on her face.

"Mrs. Ollie Mae, do you have their phone numbers?" I asked. "Yes, I have their numbers written down on a piece of paper," Mrs. Ollie Mae said. "Would you like to see them all today?" I asked. "That will be great but how are you going to do that?" Mrs. Ollie

Mae asked. "Well, I'm going to tell them all you died and we're giving them your prized possessions," I said.

Mrs. Ollie Mae shook her head. "Tammy, I don't know if you should say that. I think they will both be upset," Mrs. Ollie Mae said. "Please Mrs. Ollie Mae, I don't care if they get upset or not. Did they even know that you were in the hospital last week?" I asked. "Yes, the nurse said she informed both my children and called three of my grandchildren as well," Mrs. Ollie Mae replied.

"And neither one of them came by to see you, did they?" I asked. "No. Just my grandson Lane and his wife," Mrs. Ollie Mae replied. "Okay, well again Mrs. Ollie Mae, I don't care if they get upset or not, you just let me handle their anger. As hot and pissed off that I am right now for hearing what you just told me, then their anger isn't my concern," I said. "Okay," Mrs. Ollie Mae said, handing me the list with everyone's phone numbers on it.

I took the list from her and went to my director's Pam office and told her that I was about to cause a lot of people to get upset with me but it was time for me to do that and if she had to fire me after I'm done, then I would totally understand. Pam wanted to know what I was about to do but I told her, it was best that I didn't let her know right now, but she'll find out soon enough.

I went to the receptionist's office and made about eight phone calls and told them about Mrs. Ollie Mae's death and I heard a few screams, like they gave two cents about their mother and grandmother. I hung up the phone, with Mrs. Ollie Mae's grandson Trent, noticing how Eyvonne the receptionist was looking at me.

"Oh my God Tamara, I didn't know Mrs. Ollie Mae died last night?" Eyvonne said. "She didn't die, but if that's the only way I can get her crazy children and grandchildren here so she could see them, then that's what I'm prepared to do," I said. "Lord Tamara, those people are going to be pissed off angry with you and you could end up getting fired," Eyvonne said. "I know they will and I probably will get fired but if I can see a smile on Mrs. Ollie Mae's face, then it will be well worth it for me. I already told Pam she might want to fire me after this but that will be her decision, but please don't say anything to her or anyone else about this. I don't want anyone knowing what I'm about to do," I said. "Okay. I won't," Eyvonne said.

I went and got Mrs. Ollie Mae and told her that everyone will be here in the next two hours and she got excited and then she became sad. "It's a shame that you had to tell them that I died, in order for them to come up here," Mrs. Ollie Mae said. "Yes, that's true. I may get fired after doing this but I told my director that I don't care and it had to be done," I said. "They won't fire you sweetheart, I can promise you that," Mrs. Ollie Mae said.

"Mrs. Ollie Mae, you don't know that. You act like you have a little crystal ball or something," I said, laughing. "Tammy, I don't think you know exactly how much juice and connections I have here in little old Manning, South Carolina. Do you know Juanita Johnson and Mildred Patrick?" Mrs. Ollie Mae asked. "Yes, I do. They're the president and the vice-president of this nursing home," I said.

"That's correct and they're also my sorority sisters and great friends of mine too. So they always told me if I had any problems here at this nursing home, all I had to do is just make one phone call to them and they will take care of everything for me. I had to call them both about five times since I was here but that was it so let Pam try to fire you if she wants to, and I promise you, you'll be here after she's gone," Mrs. Ollie Mae said.

I shook my head because it was obvious that Mrs. Ollie Mae is really more than just a resident here, that lady really does have juice and power and can make stuff happen. It's just a shame that all the juice and power she has, still isn't enough to get her family to come visit her, but that's where I step in and I'm going to give her that opportunity today.

Chapter 20

Ashamed

WAITED FOR MRS. OLLIE MAE's family to all arrive in the front. I took them all in the private dining area and told them I was sorry for their loss and sorry for what they're all going through. Some of them were drying their eyes and acting like they were comforting each other, making me sick to my stomach. I texted Pam and told her to meet me in the private dining room because some BS was about to go down and I might need her assistance.

I went to Mrs. Ollie Mae's room to wheel her down to the dining room in her wheelchair. "Mrs. Ollie Mae, are you ready to see those family members that claim they love you but never come by to see you? Well today is your day to say what you have to say and get it off your chest. It's a shame I had to tell them you died and we were giving away your prized possessions for them to come to the nursing home to see you.

You know what the sad thing is, no one acted like they couldn't come like it was going to be hard for them to get here, they moved whatever they had to do in order to be able to be here, I guess because they felt like that they were getting something for free and something they didn't deserve. I know you're about to get upset with me for telling you this, but your family makes me sick to my stomach and I can't stand them," I said.

"You're okay baby and I feel your pain. I felt like this for a long time," Mrs. Ollie Mae said. I wheeled her by the dining area door. "Let me go in there and say what I have to say and I'll come back to get you," I said. "Okay," Mrs. Ollie Mae said.

Just as I was about to walk in the dining area, Pam my director came around the corner. I waited for her to get here, before we walked in together. "Tamara, I don't know what you're up to but something tells me, it's about to go down in the books as the craziest thing that has ever happened here at Creative Home Care Nursing Home," Pam said, as we both walked inside the dining area.

"Good afternoon everyone, I just want to tell you all that I'm sorry for your loss. I'm sorry that Mrs. Ollie Mae died, but you know what the sad thing is, that since I've been working here, for some reason, I have never seen any of you all here. I've heard her talk about her grandson Lane, about how he comes to visit her and calls her often. The way she talked about Lane, I thought that was her only grandchild. I would ask her if Lane was her only grandchild and she would drop her head and said "no," that she has six grandchildren

107

but Lane is the only one that takes time to come see her and calls her.

I said I'm sure your children come see you and she would say both my children live no more than ten and twenty minutes away from this nursing home and yet I never hear or see them, unless it's Christmas time and they want gifts or it's their birthday. They never pick up the phone and say "happy birthday Mama, or Happy Mother's Day Mom. I'm not pointing the finger at anyone but then again I am.

You all should be ashamed of yourselves. This lady here is my director and I'm sure that I'm going to get in trouble after this but maybe I should, but then again, I shouldn't because what I'm saying and what I did is exactly what I should've done.

When I called you all up and told you that Mrs. Ollie Mae died, I heard a few sniffles, as if you were acting like you were crying, but where were you for Christmas? Where were you for Mother's Day, or even the woman's birthday? Whenever I got her gifts and brought it to her the next day, I said did you hear from your children or your grandchildren today? She would shake her head "no," and then she would burst out crying.

I had plenty of memories with this woman as she wept, wondering what she did that was so wrong that none of her two children come by to see her, or why her grandchildren never do except Lane. I said Mrs. Ollie Mae, they must have important jobs and live in another state. She said no Tammy, both my children are retired and they live right here in Manning and Greeleyville, South Carolina. She also said all her grandchildren live in the area as well.

When she said that, my heart nearly dropped. You all live right around the area and didn't come see this woman. You all should be ashamed of yourselves and especially if you're retired. When I called you all up and told you that she died and that we were giving out her prized possessions, no one acted like they couldn't come or they were at work or anything. You all had no problem coming here then. Tell me, how would you feel to know your children put you in a place like this and just left you here and never came to check up on you?

What is ten minutes or thirty minutes of your time to say "hey Mom, or hey Grandma. I just wanted to stop by for a few minutes to see how you're doing before I have to do this or do that." That would've made all the difference to Mrs. Ollie Mae.

I just lost my mother two weeks ago from a heart attack. We spent the entire day together at my son's basketball game and later that night she sat in the recliner, and dropped to sleep and never woke back up. My mother was fifty-seven years old. I can't tell you how much I miss her and I would change places with you in a half a second to say that I have to come see my mother in a nursing home than to never see her face again. Again, you all should be ashamed of yourselves for doing that to your mother and grandmother.

I have news for all of you. Your mother died from a broken heart of not seeing her children, or her grandchildren. Not being around her family for the holidays and you all not having the decency to even call her other than to ask for gifts for yourselves or for your grandchildren. Her heart was broken a long time ago and was dead inside. She felt like no one loved her to have her in a place like this and made her feel like she was in a prison and never came to check up on her, but she didn't die physically. Your mother is still here," I said.

I opened the door and pushed Mrs. Ollie Mae inside in her wheelchair. "You're a liar! You lied about our mother being dead! I want her fired! I want her fired right now!" Mrs. Ollie Mae's son yelled. "Richie, sit your behind down and stop acting like that!" Mrs. Ollie Mae said.

"Mrs. Ollie Mae, the floor is yours," I said, giving her the microphone that we use for our meetings. "Thank you sweetheart. I know you all are upset at my nurse here, Tammy but as long as I've been a resident here, she's like a part of my family. I've shared things with her and she's shared things with me. This young lady just came back today after being out for two weeks because of her mother's death.

I was in the hospital for almost a week and no one came by to visit me, except my precious Lane. Lane came and sat with me and his lovely wife. I have five other grandsons that I didn't hear from and never hear from. My own son and daughter didn't even come check on me and see how I was doing and you both basically live in the area and only fifteen minutes away from the hospital.

When I told Tammy about how lonely I am here, it broke her heart and it pissed her off. She just lost her mother and she's not coming back, but you all still have me but you act like I'm dead or at least dead to you. You might say she went too far but I think she did exactly what she should've done in order to get my children and my grandchildren here, and all of you live in the same area. She's right, you all should be ashamed of yourselves for treating me this way.

There's an old saying, I used to hear older people say all the time when I was younger, "don't wait until I'm dead to give me my flowers, because I can't smell them then, but give them to me while I'm alive and right here." I'm still here but you act like I'm dead.

Tammy didn't tell you I was dead, she told you I died. I died in my heart, because my heart can't take it anymore of how you all treat me. My spirit died along with my broken heart and I've felt this way for a long time now, because I still have family that act like I'm dead and have acted like that since I've been here at this nursing home. Some days, I don't want to live, knowing that the only reason you all would come to my funeral is to see if I left you something in my will and that's horrible.

Richie and Donna, whatever I've done to you for you two to treat me like this, I'm sorry. I'm so, so sorry. Whatever I did to my grandchildren, other than Lane, then I'm sorry to you as well. Please forgive me," Mrs. Ollie Mae said, as she burst out in tears.

I reached down and hugged her and kissed her on her cheek. "I love you Mrs. Ollie Mae," I said. "I love you too sweetheart," Mrs. Ollie Mae said. I walked out of the dining area and went to grab my things, because I knew I was fired for what I did.

I grabbed my things and as I was about to walk out of the building to go to my car, I heard Pam calling my name. Pam was running down the hallway. Pam is a plus size lady so I walked towards her so she didn't have to run far. "Yes Pam," I said. "You know I have grounds to terminate you for what you did because it was totally unethical and stands against our mission but I'm not going to do that.

Mrs. Ollie Mae told me, I better not try to fire you because she would come for my job next. In all twenty-five years that I've been here, I've never seen anyone do what you did today. What you did was definitely necessary and you shouldn't have to do that to get someone's family to come visit them at a place they already don't want to be in the first place.

I promise you Mrs. Ollie Mae is never going to forget this for as long as she lives. God bless you

Tamara and I'm so thankful that I have someone like you working here. Your attitude and caring heart is what Creative Home Care Nursing Home needs. So put your stuff down, you're not going anywhere," Pam said, as she reached out and gave me a hug.

I was about to go to the nursing station when, Mrs. Ollie Mae's son and daughter came walking towards me. Now it's been a long time since I had to fight besides Steven but I promise I haven't forgot if they were trying to find out.

"Ms. Tamara, we want to say thank you. It took us thinking our mother had died for us to run up here like that, when she's been alive the entire time and we never made time for her. Sometimes it takes a stranger to point out the obvious to us and you certainly did that. Thank you so much and we definitely appreciate you for everything you've done."

I sat down at my desk before doing my rounds. I had to reflect back on today and what all happened. When I first got to work, I was so busy in my own pain and still grieving that I had to put my own problems aside and God saw fit for me to help this family out. I sure hope they do better by Mrs. Ollie Mae, because you only have one mother and when she's gone, all the crying, screaming, regret, and pain, won't bring her back. Once they close their eyes for the last time, that's it.

Chapter 21

I Can Leave Now

JUST WAVED AT THE LAST of Mrs. Ollie Mae's grandchildren, that just left the nursing home. They spent most of the day with her and she really enjoyed it. She couldn't stop smiling and that smile looked good on her. I got up to check on her to see if she was okay and enjoyed her day today.

I knocked on Mrs. Ollie Mae's door and walked on inside. "Hey there pretty lady," I said, sitting beside her bed. "Hey Tammy. How are you?" Mrs. Ollie Mae asked. "I'm fine. Today was a great day?" I said. "It certainly was Tammy. My family was here and I was able to enjoy them all thanks to you.

It's a shame that you had to lie in order to get them here. Isn't it something how people want to come around when they think that there's something in it for them? Tammy baby, my time is winding down pretty quickly. If I'm here another week, it's only because God isn't ready for me yet. Not because of what the doctors have said to me. Time isn't on my side and what you showed me today, just allowed me to see that my family is only after material things, because had you not said what you said, they would've never come up here.

Look Tammy, I'm a very wealthy woman but my family doesn't know how wealthy I am. I have my son and daughter getting ten thousand dollars in my will and my six grandchildren to all get five thousand each," Mrs. Ollie Mae said.

"Okay, so Lane will be getting what your other grandchildren are getting?" I asked. "Yes but I have a special reading later that evening for Lane and for you," Mrs. Ollie Mae said. "Me? Why me?" I asked. "Tammy, you're more than my nurse, you're family to me and family doesn't have to be blood related." "Mrs. Ollie Mae, you don't have to do that," I said. "I know I don't, but I'm going to do that. Trust me sweet heart, you'll never have to work again in your life," Mrs. Ollie Mae said.

I was actually speechless. "Tammy, my lawyer will get in touch with you and will read out the remaining of my will to you and my grandson. No one in the family knows about a second reading, so please don't say anything to anyone about it," Mrs. Ollie Mae said. "I wouldn't do that," I said. "You know when it's my time to go, I have everything planned out. I already have my obituary written out, to the color of my dress, and I even picked out my casket."

"Excuse me," I said about to walk out of Mrs. Ollie Mae's room because I felt the tears already coming down my face. "Tammy, I know this is going to be rough on you to have just lost your Mom and to be losing me soon too, but you'll be okay. I want to tell you to keep on doing what you're doing with this job. You're doing a fantastic job and I'm so proud of you, but Tammy you'll soon have a turnover that's going to shake up everything in your life. Everything you thought was gone in your life, hasn't left you for good. The devil is busy and he's seeking who he can devour and destroy.

Don't you let the devil win by giving up, because when it's all over with, you're going to be the one to come out on top. Don't give up Tammy, don't give up the fight. The Bible says, "that the race is not to the swift or the battle to the strong, but he that shall endure unto the end, he will be saved."

Tammy, when you're stuck in between a rock and a hard place, remember the word and "lean not on your own understanding, in all your ways, submit to him and he will make your path straight." God will give you the desires of your heart, just trust and believe that he will," Mrs. Ollie Mae said.

"Mrs. Ollie Mae, what does all that mean?" I asked. "You just have to wait and see Tammy but trust me, when this thing that you're going to go through is staring you in the face, remember to trust in him and in the word, because he'll never put more on you than you can bear. The devil is busy, especially when he thinks that no one has your back.

Look, give me that notepad off the night stand and a pen. I handed Mrs. Ollie Mae the notepad and the pen she asked for. "Please give me my cell phone," Mrs. Ollie Mae asked. I gave her, her cell phone, as she wrote down a number and a name on the notepad and handed it to me.

I looked at the name and number on the piece of paper. The name read "Lawrence Collins," I wonder who in the world is this person? "Mrs. Ollie Mae, who is Lawrence Collins?" I asked. "He's my great-nephew. My sister's grandson. Lawrence is an attorney and something tells me, you're going to need that. Make sure to put that in a safe place, that you can always go back to," Mrs. Ollie Mae said. "I sure will," I replied.

"Tammy, you know I had a wonderful day with my family and I got to spend time with you as well. You know, I think God was using you as a vessel to get all my family here today but I needed you here to do that. Sweetheart, it was no accident that you came back today on this special day of all days," Mrs. Ollie Mae said. "Why today, Mrs. Ollie Mae?" I asked.

"Do you know that song "Soon I will be done, with the troubles of this world?" Mrs. Ollie Mae asked, ignoring my question. "I think so, but I don't want to sing it, because I know what that means?" I said, as my tears started rushing down my face. "Well Tammy, it's going to happen either way, at least I can give you a proper good-bye. God is ready to take me on home," Mrs. Ollie Mae said.

I walked up to her and hugged her tightly and kissed her on the cheek. "I love you with all my heart

Mrs. Ollie Mae. You mean the world to me," I said. "I love you too Tammy and you mean the world to me as well. You be strong and you take care of that son of yours. He's going to definitely make you proud. I'm so happy and blessed to have had a nurse like you, that not only just thought of this place as a job, but you carried it in your heart as well. This place needs more nurses and caring people like you," Mrs. Ollie Mae said.

I just smiled and sat in the recliner beside Mrs. Ollie Mae, while she laid in the bed and I held her hand. "Mrs. Ollie Mae, now I'm no CeCe Winans or Yolanda Adams or anything like that, but I can carry a tune though and that's it," I said. "That's okay baby. I just want to hear the words to it," Mrs. Ollie Mae said.

I closed my eyes to let God use me as I ministered this song that was probably going to be my last request of Mrs. Ollie Mae. As I started singing, the words just naturally flowed off my lips. I felt a cold chill that came over my body, like something had just lifted off of me. Maybe that was God wanting me to know he was here because I definitely could feel his presence in this room.

I was singing my heart out, while the tears were constantly coming down my face. I heard the door to the room open but I wouldn't open my eyes to see who came inside. I was just letting God use me through this song. Mrs. Ollie Mae said our timing may not be God's timing but he knows what he's doing.

As I was in the middle of the song, I felt the life left from Mrs. Ollie Mae's hand, and I knew she was going on to be with the Lord and has left her earthly home. I ended the song, and opened my eyes to see everyone standing in the doorway, just listening and looking, as Mrs. Ollie Mae just transitioned on the other side.

I looked at her as she laid so peacefully with her eyes closed and I leaned over and kissed her on her cheek. "Take your rest Mrs. Ollie Mae, your work here on earth is done and now you're getting your reward. I will miss you dearly," I said, walking out the room.

Chapter 22

He Asked Me Out

IT'S BEEN A LONG WEEK and to return back to work, only to witness one of my favorite residents that's been like a mother to me, pass away, with me holding her hand. I must say Mrs. Ollie Mae got to do everything she wanted to do today, including spending time with her family.

I worked over today since one of the RN's wouldn't be in today. I called and checked on Calvin to see what he was doing. He told me that he was home watching TV. Calvin was still training with Dammon, when he wasn't at basketball practice. I picked up some Chinese food and brought it home.

I put the food down and went and checked in on Calvin in his bedroom. Calvin was on his bed, doing his homework, with his headphones on. I swear this boy, someone could break in the house and rob us and Calvin would never know, unless he walked out and actually saw them doing it.

I popped Calvin on the behind, as he jumped up. "Oh hey Mom. When did you get here?" Calvin asked.

"Boy, if you take those headphones off your head, you'll know if someone is in the house or something," I said.

Calvin got up and hugged and kissed me on the cheek. "Mom, how was your first day back to work?" Calvin asked. "Baby, at first it was okay and then I had to get nasty and then I ended up crying the rest of the night," I said. "You started thinking about Grandma?" Calvin asked.

I sat down on Calvin's bed beside him and told him all about my crazy day. "Oh Lord Mom, that's crazy. I'm so sorry you had to go through all that. I was hoping that we both would end up having a good day, but I guess that didn't happen for you," Calvin said. "I know baby, but I'm so glad it's over with now," I replied.

"I'm hungry Mom. What are we eating for dinner?" Calvin asked. "I picked up some Chinese and it's on the table now," I said. "Okay, because a brother is hungry and ready to eat," Calvin said. "Well, go wash your hands and we can eat then," I said.

Calvin and I had dinner and it felt strange sitting at the table eating without Mom sitting here with us. I think this is the first time we sat here at our table and ate since Mom died. This was always a tradition at our house to sit at the dinner table and fellowship with one another.

Calvin told me how well he was doing in basketball and that he had a game with Scott's Branch this Friday.

I told him I would definitely be there, once I got off from work.

After dinner, I told Calvin to get back to his homework. He went on in his room. I decided to pour up a glass of wine and started listening to some music. I was enjoying the voice of Musiq Soulchild, when I heard a knock on the front door. I stood up and went to the door. I looked out the window and saw it was Dammon. "Who is it?" I asked, making sure It was Dammon's voice, in case my eyes were playing tricks on me. "It's me, Dammon," he said.

I opened the door, "Hey Dammon. I didn't know that you were coming over tonight?" I said. "I wasn't planning to but Calvin left his jacket in my car," Dammon said, as he handed it to me. "I swear that boy would lose his darn head if it wasn't attached to his body," I said. "Ah, ease up off my boy. You know he has a lot on his mind with basketball and holding the girls down at school," Dammon said.

"Dammon, please come in. I'm sorry for my rudeness," I said. Dammon came inside and sat down on the couch. "I'm having a glass of wine. Would you like a glass?" I asked. "Sure, I'll have a glass," Dammon said.

I went to the kitchen and grabbed another wine glass out of the cabinet and poured him a glass and handed it to him. "So how's your night so far?" I asked. "It's going pretty good. I haven't been doing much but just chilling around the house," Dammon said.

"Dammon, I don't know much about you at all. Are you married and do you have children?" I asked. "No, I'm divorced and I don't have any children. My wife and never had any children together.

I guess that's why I have so many guys that I mentor and coach, to fill that empty void of me not having any children of my own. I feel like a father figure in their lives, especially for the ones that don't have a father around," Dammon said.

I couldn't believe that someone as handsome as Dammon isn't married or dating someone, but then again I'm just assuming that he's not, acting like I know this man's business at all. "Dammon, you better not stay over here too long, I don't want your girlfriend coming over here, trying to track you down," I said, laughing. "Please, I don't have a girlfriend. I must be too ugly for anyone to want to date me because the women I try to talk to, don't want to talk back," Dammon said.

I shook my head at Dammon's comment but I didn't believe that for one minute. "Now someone as pretty as you, I know you have men lined up trying to date you," Dammon said. "Well, I do have a few men that have showed interest, but I don't think they want a relationship though. All they want is what they want at the moment and that's it," I said.

Dammon shook his head. "I guess things are still the same way and haven't changed at all," Dammon said. "You probably was worse huh? I mean, a player, player," I said, laughing. "No, I wasn't like that at all,"

Dammon said. "Well, maybe you're an exception but a lot of men are like that," I said.

"Well maybe you haven't met the right man yet. You had a bad marriage but not all men are bad because your husband was. I wish I had a woman like you Tamara. I promise you, I would be good to you. You think you would give a guy like me a chance?" Dammon asked. "I definitely would," I said. "So would you let me take you out on a date?" Dammon asked. "I think I would like that but I need to make sure Calvin wouldn't have a problem with it. You are his coach and for the longest it's been just me and my son," I said.

"That's understandable but even if he says no, you don't let a child dictate who you're going to date or who you want to be with, because he is still a child and we're the adults," Dammon said.

Dammon is absolutely right. I don't need Calvin's permission to date anyone, but I do want to have his input before Dammon and I try to pursue each other. I guess I just want to make sure he's okay with it. "He just lost his grandmother and he needs to know that I'm here for him," I said. "I totally understand. Well, I'll let you go talk to him and you just tell me what you decide," Dammon said.

I got up and walked Dammon to the door. "I hope Calvin will be okay with it because I would definitely love to take you out and get to know you a little better than just being your son's basketball coach," Dammon said, as he leaned over and kissed me on the cheek.

I closed the door behind Dammon and went and knocked on Calvin's door. "Come in," Calvin said. I opened the door and walked in Calvin's room. "Hey Mom, what's up?" Calvin asked. "Dammon brought your jacket by that you left in his car," I said. "Oh dang. I totally forgot I left it in his car," Calvin said.

"Oh okay. Look, how would you feel about Dammon and I going out on a date? He asked me out when he dropped your jacket off. Would you be okay with that?" I asked. "Mom, it wouldn't bother me at all. I just want you to get out of this house before you slip into a deep depression. You know depression can slip up on you when you least expect it. I don't want that for you," Calvin said.

I listened to my baby's words and what he said, definitely made sense. Dammon and I are just going on a date and that's it. It's not like he's asked me for my hand in marriage or anything like that, so getting out will definitely do me some good.

Chapter 23

To Us

TODAY WAS EXTREMELY HARD FOR me to be at work and not see Mrs. Ollie Mae's beautiful face. I caught myself going straight to her room, when Kay, one of the RN's stopped me before I could open her room door. As soon as she called my name, "Tamara," I froze and then I burst out crying. I swear it's like losing my mother all over again.

Today was definitely one of those days that I really had to plaster a fake smile on my face, and pretend that I was alright, when I knew I wasn't. Pam told me that she's so glad that I got Mrs. Ollie Mae's family all there yesterday, so she could see them all one last time.

I just got off from work and was heading to my car. I swung by Calvin's school to pick him up after basketball practice. I swear, I'll be so glad when this boy starts driving. I think I'll give him Mom's car when he's old enough to drive.

I swear life knows it can be unpredictable. If anyone was to tell me that my mother would no longer be here, I would call them a liar and tell them my mother wouldn't dare leave me alone by myself. Every time I turn the radio on and a song would come on that Mom liked, I just smiled to myself and then I would start crying.

Calvin definitely misses his grandmother as well. Last night, I got up to go to the restroom and I heard him in his room, crying and saying how he was going to make his grandmother so proud of him. It took everything inside me not to go in Calvin's room and hold him in my arms but I knew he needed that time to grieve alone.

Calvin got in the car. "Hey Mom. How are you?" Calvin asked. "I'm fine sweetheart. How are you?" I asked. "I'm okay. You know every day I come out the school, expecting Grandma to be here waiting on me and tell me, "boy you know I'm not going anywhere, until you make it to the NBA," Calvin said, trying to crack a smile beyond his tears. "I miss Grandma so much Mom. I miss how Grandma would get up an hour earlier on work days and make us breakfast and we all sat and had breakfast together," Calvin said, rubbing his eyes.

I was so full that I couldn't even speak. I had to just sit in the parking lot of the school and cry my eyes out, as Calvin did the same. "Mom, I'm so sorry to make you sad. I didn't mean to do that," Calvin said. "It's okay son, it's not your fault. I've been an emotional wreck all day today. If I wasn't crying for Mom, I was crying because I missed Mrs. Ollie Mae."

I don't think I went through an entire hour today without crying. I know eventually time will heal all wounds and it's going to take some time to do just that. I think I was okay enough to drive home, since we only lived about twelve minutes from the school.

"Do you have homework son?" I asked. "No homework today, "Calvin said. "Oh okay. How about hotdogs and fries for dinner tonight? You know I'm going out with Dammon tonight?" I said. "I forgot all about that Mom," Calvin replied.

Dammon picked me up at seven-o'clock and we went to Longhorn for dinner. It wasn't crowded, which is definitely a surprise, since it's normally always packed. Dammon and I talked and had interesting conversation. I will admit that Dammon isn't my initial type but he's definitely a handsome guy.

He reminds me of Tyrese Gibson but he's a little heavier, weighing about two hundred and twenty pounds and about six feet tall. He's just a little on the thicker side then what I'm used to. "How's your food?" Dammon asked. "It's good and yours?" I asked.

I noticed how Dammon was staring at me and I was trying not to let it make me feel uncomfortable but it was definitely giving me some stalker type of vibe from him. I had to say something because he's getting on my nerves now with this staring mess. "Dammon, why are you staring at me like that?" I asked. "I'm sorry Tamara. I don't mean to stare. You're just so beautiful, that's all," Dammon said. "Thank you," I replied, with a smile.

After dinner, Dammon took me to the fair. I don't think I've ever been to a fair on a first date before and it was quite different. It was actually nice and Dammon brought the inner child out of me and I even got on a few rides with him, even though I'm terrified of roller coasters and rides like that; but for some reason, I felt safe with Dammon.

Dammon grabbed my hand and smiled. "Are you having fun?" Dammon asked. "Yes, I am," I said. "I'm glad," Dammon replied, as we walked around the fair and enjoyed our date together. At first I was hoping that our date would hurry up and end so I could get back home and I wouldn't go out with him again, but now I don't know. I think I just had to give our date a chance and give Dammon a chance as well. I'm so glad I did because I really appreciate the thought of him thinking outside the box and doing something a little different than the average dinner and a movie. I think I will go on another date with him, if he was to ask me because I definitely had fun tonight.

Chapter 24

The Will

TODAY WAS THE DAY THAT they laid Mrs. Ollie Mae to rest. The family asked if I would like to say a few words and I told them I wasn't strong enough to do that, especially after just losing my mother as well. Mrs. Donna, Mrs. Ollie Mae's daughter told me she totally forgot about that and that just my presence would be good enough.

I thanked her and told her I would definitely be there. The church was a big beautiful church, but there were only about fifty people here, outside of the family. The choir sang "Amazing Grace," and one of the deacons said a prayer. The Pastor came up to deliver the eulogy. Lord, this was the fastest funeral I ever attended in my entire life. The entire funeral was no longer than twenty minutes.

If Mrs. Ollie Mae was black, it would probably take longer to get the people inside the church than the time her entire funeral lasted. I guess the amount of time of the funeral reflected on Mrs. Ollie Mae because she definitely was a no playing around type of woman.

She said what she said and meant every word she said. They always said that you should never get attached to any of the residents at the nursing home but I couldn't help it. Mrs. Ollie Mae had a contagious spirit that made you fall in love with her, but if she didn't like you, she definitely made it known. So either you loved her, or you hated her, but either one, she didn't care.

I can't speak for anyone at Creative Home Care Nursing Home but I loved and adored Mrs. Ollie Mae. She always teased me and told me I was the black daughter she always wanted. When she said that I would burst out laughing.

If it wasn't for my son, I don't know what I would do. I feel so empty now. My mom is gone and Mrs. Ollie Mae as well, and just when I got back to work that Monday too. God knew exactly what he was doing. He allowed me to come back to work that day, round up all her family so she could spend that last day with them and she knew she was able to see me back to work and her family that one last time and then she was ready to leave us.

Mrs. Ollie Mae didn't seem scared or anything, she was content with how things were going to go and it was well with her soul. Mrs. Ollie Mae left this place in a good mood because she was saying goodbye to the troubles of this world and she was going on home to be with the Lord. I didn't know then why she wanted me to sing that song, but now I know and I'm glad I was able to sing it while she was transitioning to her new heavenly home. "Sleep well Mrs. Ollie Mae, you have finished the course."

I went around and told Mr. Richie and Mrs. Donna and her grandchildren that I was leaving and to take care. Lane was pretty shaken up, and when I hugged him, he hugged me tightly and thanked me for everything I did for his grandmother. I smiled and told him he was very welcome.

As I was about to leave the funeral, a young lady approached me. "Hello, I'm Amanda Elliott and I'm Mrs. Ollie Mae's attorney. I'm sure she told you that she left you something in her will as well as her grandson Lane. She wanted me to do a private, separate will for just you two," Amanda said. "Yes she told me before she died," I replied.

"Okay good. I'm going to meet the family immediately after the services and then I can meet you and Lane at my office around one-thirty if that's okay?" Ms. Amanda said. "Yes, that will be fine," I replied. "Good, here's my card and my address is on there," Ms. Amanda said.

I left the church and got a two-piece meal from KFC. I went home and ate since I only live around the corner from the church. I'm glad I took off today because something told me I would be no good to attend Mrs. Ollie Mae's funeral and then turn around and go to work afterwards.

I finished eating and brushed my teeth to make sure I don't have any food particles between them. I changed my clothes to get out of these heels and what I wore to the funeral. I wanted to put on something a little more comfortable so I put on my gray Nike sweat suit, that Calvin got me last year for my birthday.

I pulled up to Ms. Amanda's office and as I was getting out the car, Lane pulled up right beside me. "Hello, Tamara. How are you?" Lane asked, as he extended his hand toward me. I could tell Lane was definitely grieving Mrs. Ollie Mae's death, because his eyes were red and quite puffy, as if he's been crying all day. I know his grandmother's death is really affecting him because she really did love him. Mrs. Ollie Mae said that Lane was the only one that gave two cents about her and she was going to definitely make sure he was well taken care of.

"Hello Lane," I said, ignoring his handshake and giving him a hug. "I'm so sorry for your loss Lane. I know you and your grandmother were extremely close. She talked about you all the time, of how proud she was of you. Your grandmother was definitely a very sweet woman and I love and miss her very much," I said.

Lane nodded his head and tried to muster up a smile but I could tell he was just trying to keep it together. "I sure hope Ms. Amanda does this quickly, because I want to put this behind me and move forward," Lane said. "I'm sure you do," I replied.

Lane and I both went inside the building and followed her to her office. Mrs. Amanda sat down at her desk, while we sat down next to each other. "First of all,

I would like to give you both my condolences on the loss of Mrs. Ollie Mae. She was definitely a beautiful and loving woman. She was definitely a one of a kind woman. She also didn't like confusion and foolishness, so that's why she wanted me to do a separate reading of the will with you both. No one knew that Mrs. Ollie Mae was quite a wealthy woman. Not even her own children.

Mrs. Ollie Mae knew that her children and the other grandchildren were only about money and material things; that's why she had me give them what they got earlier after the service and had me do this one separately. Lane, this is your check and Tamara, this is your check. You are to never tell a soul how much you got as long as you live. Mrs. Ollie Mae also left a sizeable amount to the nursing home as well, because she said she enjoyed the people there and the staff were definitely nice to her.

Lane looked in his envelope and his mouth dropped. "Oh my God Grandma. You left me twenty million dollars," Lane said, in disbelief. I didn't want to open mine, especially in front of Lane. There was just no telling how he would react, especially since I'm not blood related. He might send some of his friends or family members after me and I'm not having that. My mom didn't raise me to be anyone's fool or dummy. Some things you just have to keep to yourself and this was definitely one of them.

"Are you going to open yours?" Ms. Amanda asked. "No I'm not. I'll do that later," I said. "Ah come on Tamara. I said how much mine was," Lane said, like I owed him to tell him my amount. "No. I'll open it with my son later on. Ms. Amanda, is there anything else you need from me?" I asked. "No, that's it," Ms. Amanda said.

I reached over and hugged Lane again. "Lane, you take care of yourself and God bless you and your family," I said. "Thank you Tamara and you do the same as well," Lane replied. "Thank you for your help Ms. Amanda," I said, extending my hand towards her. "You are quite welcome. You take care Tamara," Ms. Amanda said, as I left her office.

I called the school and told them that I'm picking my son Calvin up for early dismissal. Calvin only had one class left so he should be okay since he's a straight "A" student.

I pulled up to the school and went to the office and waited for them to call Calvin. I know he's going to be surprised but I wanted to open this envelope in front of him. "Hey Mom," Calvin said, giving me a hug. "Hey sweetheart," I said. "What are you doing here? Did something happen?" Calvin asked. "I'll tell you when we get in the car," I said, signing the book for Calvin's early dismissal.

Calvin and I got in the car and he kept asking me what's going on, because I don't normally just pick him up early from school, unless he has some kind of appointment or something.

"Sweetheart, you know I went to Mrs. Ollie Mae's funeral today right?" I said. "Yes, I remember. I hope it wasn't too sad?" Calvin asked. "No, it wasn't but I had to come back later for the reading of the will. They had a will read for the family and then a separate will was done from Mrs. Ollie Mae's grandson and myself, so her other family didn't know what she left us.

When the lawyer gave me my envelope, I refused to look at it unless I was doing it with you so this is the envelope right here," I said, holding up the envelope so Calvin could see it. "Well go ahead and open it Mom," Calvin said, with excitement in his voice, like he wanted to snatch the envelope from my hand and open it up himself.

I laughed at Calvin's reaction and decided to open the envelope. My mouth dropped when I saw the check that was presented to me for the amount of twenty-million dollars. There was something folded up on a piece of paper that I took out the envelope to look at.

"Mom, I know that's not how much I think it is? Did Mrs. Ollie Mae leave you twenty-million dollars?" Calvin asked. "Yes she did," I said, still in shock myself.

I opened the piece of paper and read what was on it. Mrs. Ollie Mae left me ten acres of land in Summerton, South Carolina. I saw she had written a little note to me.

"Hey my beautiful black nurse,

I wanted to just say thank you for making my time wonderful at Creative Home Care Nursing Home, a pleasant stay. I was never around my real family there but you were like a daughter to me. Thank you for making my last few years a pleasant one. I love you and I pray that you find the happiness you deserve because Lord knows you deserve it. I love you my beautiful black nurse.

Love Mrs. Ollie Mae,"

I had tears in my eyes and not only was I grateful for the money and land that Mrs. Ollie Mae willed to me, but I'm blessed to have met and loved a woman such as wonderful as her. Mrs. Ollie Mae, I love and miss you so much and thank you from the bottom of my heart for everything. You were so right when you said, "that you don't have to be blood related to be family," and I certainly agree with that phrase.

Chapter 25

Not A Baby Anymore

I SAT WATCHING MY BABY SHOOT his free throws after being fouled by Scott's Branch. Calvin has already scored thirty points and it's only the second quarter of the game. Calvin has been offered by five different colleges a full scholarship in basketball. He talked with six basketball coaches last week and the week before he had seven. I told Calvin I feel like his personal secretary writing all these messages for him.

Calvin laughed and told me he knew I liked to do it. I laughed but to be honest I enjoy it. I enjoy seeing the smile on his face when he tells me to guess what college wants to meet him this week.

I joked and told Calvin he's like a celebrity and everyone wants him. He still practices with Dammon, and Dammon and I are still dating. It's been four years now and he's not worrying about asking me to marry him and I'm not worried about a proposal at all. I told Dammon as long as we love each other, then we don't need to get married for that. Dammon agreed and told me there was no pressure on us getting married since he was divorced and I'm divorced as well.

Dammon doesn't know about the money that was willed to me by both my mother or Mrs. Ollie Mae and that wasn't something I was willing to share with him. I put two million in a college trust fund for Calvin back then so he'll be able to live off the interest for the rest of his life, if he doesn't make it in the NBA like he talks about doing. He kept saying he was going to buy me a big house but I told him I'm content living in my mother's house, because I have such wonderful fond memories here. I feel close to my mother living here.

The game was over and Calvin's school ended up beating Scott's Branch by two points, 90-88. Calvin ended up scoring forty-eight points with twenty-two rebounds. Calvin came straight up to me. "Hey Mom. Did you see your son killing it on the basketball court?" Calvin asked, cheesing from ear to ear. "I see you son. My little NBA player," I said, laughing.

"Calvin, this is Rolland Marrow of the Boston Celtics," Dammon said. "Oh wow. How are you doing Mr. Marrow?" Calvin asked. "I'm doing well. Calvin and Mrs. Martin, I would like to sit down and talk to you about Calvin's future. This year the NBA is drafting high school students straight into the NBA if they can show us they have what it takes to be an NBA star.

If Calvin were to sign up with us he would get a five-million-dollar initial sign on bonus and fifteen million after his first year. After what we have seen this week, we are willing to make an offer today." "Mr. Marrow thank you, but I think we should hear from other coaches and see if any other NBA teams want to sign my son," I said.

"Well ma'am, we can guarantee that Calvin probably won't get another contract as generous as ours, so I think we should sign now and get him on board," Mr. Marrow said. "Mr. Marrow do you have a card? But again this will have to be a decision that my son and I will have to sit down and discuss together," I said.

"Okay ma'am, I understand. Here's my card. Please get in touch with me as soon as possible," Mr. Marrow said. "Thank you Mr. Marrow," I said. As I was walking off I saw Dammon back there talking to Mr. Marrow.

Calvin and I got in the car. "Mom, you were a little rude back there to Mr. Marrow," Calvin said. "Well, I wasn't trying to be son. I just want what's best for you. I want you to go to college," I said. "Mom, you are my mother and I respect what you tell me and your opinion but the bottom line is, this isn't your decision to make. I'm the one that's out here busting my behind off like that on the court to have a bright career for myself. Respectfully Mom," Calvin said.

"Baby, I know this your decision and your decision alone but from my opinion, I want you to go to college. Not only can you play basketball, but you're good in all sports, but you're academically smart as well. Do you know how many athletes would die to be as smart and intelligent as you? Son, you got a 1560 on your SAT and the highest score is 1600. You also got a 30 on the ACT and the highest is a 36.

Sweetheart, you are definitely no dummy. I know you can make tons of money playing in the NBA but I just want you to be careful and not put all your eggs into one basket. An education is something you can always fall back on.

Look okay, Mr. Marrow offered you five-million dollars and fifteen million after your first year. What if the Lakers offer you eight million and twenty-five million after your first year and a few days later the Heat offer you ten million and twenty-five or thirty million after your first year?

Calvin, sometimes you have to kind of weigh your options out instead of jumping straight into a contract or dealing with the first person that approaches you. Give it at least until next week and if you don't hear back from any other NBA coaches, then you call Mr. Marrow back," I said.

"Mom, that makes sense what you're telling me but I just don't want to miss an opportunity that's knocking on my door," Calvin said. "You're right son but look at it this way, you're a realtor and you saw an old house that you know you can fix up and flip it. You bought a house for twenty-thousand and you pay someone fifteen thousand to fix it up so you spent thirty-five-thousand on the house total.

So you got the house the way you want it and you sell it. Son, what you want to do is sell it for way more, than what you put in the house so you want a big profit. You want to sell the house for about one hundred and sixty thousand. You want that to be your bottom base price, meaning you won't take less than that but you want to have a price that you can play around with.

I would do two-hundred thousand dollars, that way if a client says, I want to negotiate to one-ninety, and another client wants to do one hundred and eighty, and the third wants to do one-hundred and seventy. You go with the highest bid which is one-hundred and ninety. Now you can come back to this potential buyer and say, "sorry sir, but I have a client that is willing to pay two-hundred and ten thousand for the house", knowing that isn't true but that's a chance you're taking by doing that. It may work or it may not work but at least you tried. That's called bluffing.

Son, everyone does it but you just have to know how to do it. So just be patient and see, you could get a much better offer than what the Celtics are offering you. Calvin, I'm your Mom and I only want what's best for you but this is your decision. Just know I love you and I'm behind you one-hundred percent," I said.

"Thanks Mom. I value your opinion and I'm definitely going to look at all my options," Calvin said. "Well good son. That's all I want you to do. Look, keep an eye on Dammon too. Let me know if he's trying to pressure you into signing on with the Celtics. I saw him talking to Mr. Marrow after you two talked and he was getting a little too cozy up with him, and shaking his hand, like he was trying to make some kind of arrangement with him. I wouldn't be surprised if Mr. Marrow promised Dammon a few million if he could get you to sign on with them.

Just keep your eyes open. I'm sure with his line of work, he's probably been doing that to a lot of the young guys he's been training and helping to get to the NBA. You can't trust no one but your mother," I said.

Calvin looked shocked but I think he knows that people aren't to be trusted like that anymore. "Son, you have to be very careful these days because people are jealous when they see you constantly in the papers and on the news and got all kinds of scouts behind you. Jealousy comes in many different shapes and sizes as well as faces. Everyone you thought had your back, don't be surprised if they start turning their backs on you. Don't be surprised when people all of a sudden want to be your friend, that acted like they wouldn't give you the time of day in school or around the block. Don't be going to little parties and meeting these little fast behind girls.

You'll be surprised what these little fast behind girls will do just to trap you into a place you don't want to be, like an unexpected pregnancy or something," I said. "Mom, you watch too many Lifetime movies," Calvin said, laughing. "You can say what you want but mark my words son, there are people that are out there, just waiting on your success because they think that will be a come up for them as well. Just watch and see," I said.

Calvin acts so naïve sometimes, like everyone is so innocent and doesn't have hidden agendas but he'll have to find out for himself. I can only tell him that people aren't always who they appear to be, but he'll have to see that on his own.

I swear it seems like only yesterday when Shemika asked me to watch Calvin that night, while they went to the movies and they never came back. Now that little one-year-old little boy that I raised and adopted as my son, isn't a little boy anymore. He's almost a grown man, and making grown man decisions. Time please slow down for just a little while and let me enjoy my son before he feels like he's too old to hang out with his mom anymore.

Chapter 26

I Have To Tell Him

AFTER DINNER CALVIN TOLD ME that he's going to wait on going to college and he's going to go ahead and pursue his basketball career in the NBA, while he has a shot. I told him even though I didn't like his decision, I had to accept it.

They showed clips of my baby on the news all night of his big game today. Calvin was dunking and slamming all over those guys and I couldn't be any prouder of my baby while he was doing what he loves to do. I can't believe that I raised a basketball player that may be going to the NBA. I'm so happy and proud that I can go on the tallest building and scream my lungs out, telling the world that my son is on his way to the NBA. How many parents can actually say that?

I got up and went to Calvin's room, and he was doing his homework, with his headphones on his head. I knocked on his door and then walked on in and sat on his bed. Calvin noticed me and took off his headphones and sat up. "Hey Mom. What's up?" Calvin said, with a big Kool-Aid smile.

"Hey son. We need to talk," I said. Calvin looked at me, with a serious look on his face, like he knew what I had to tell him was very important, which it definitely is. I had Calvin's undivided attention. I knew it was time for me to tell my baby the truth that I held from him for over sixteen years.

I hope he won't be too upset since I waited all these years to tell him but he needs to know the truth. "Calvin, I want to tell you a story about two best friends. The two young ladies' names were Shemika and Tamara. They were both the same age and were the very best of friends. These girls did everything together, but one girl Shemika was a little more out there and more daring than Tamara was.

Shemika gave birth and had a son that she loved but she always threw him off on Tamara to watch him, while Shemika did whatever she wanted to do. Now Tamara lived with her mother so she didn't live by herself. Tamara loved children but she couldn't have children of her own, because of a medical procedure that she had years ago, that damaged a part of her body.

Shemika knew that about her best friend Tamara, and believe me, she took advantage of that because Shemika knew that her best friend Tamara, loved her son very much and would do anything for him.

One particular night, Shemika and her boyfriend wanted to go to the movies to get out of the house for a change. Tamara agreed to watch her godson, Shemika's child until they come back from the movies, about three hours later. Shemika and her boyfriend never showed up within those hours to get her son. Shemika was fully aware that Tamara worked third shift and was off that night, so that's why she asked her in the first place.

Tamara called and called and never got an answer from Shemika, or heard from her boyfriend again. That next night, Tamara had to go to work so she kept calling and calling Shemika to come get her son, but Shemika never answered her phone.

Tamara and her mother talked, and her mother told her to go to Shemika's mother's house to talk to her so she could take the little boy. Tamara did that but the mother wouldn't take the little boy in. The mother suggested that Tamara go talk to her older daughter to see if she would take the child in but the older sister didn't want to get involved because she knew her sister was a walking time bomb and there was no telling when or if she would ever come back.

Calvin, Tamara had to call the authorities and Child Protective Services, and they wanted to take the little boy away but Tamara told them she'd rather keep the little boy than to see him grow up in the system. They agreed and allowed Tamara to be the little boy's foster mother.

Tamara has heard of too many horrible stories of children being in the system so Tamara was able to raise the little boy with her mother's help. Tamara raised the little boy up into a fine young man. Shemika never came back to check on the little boy to see how he's doing or anything.

Now Shemika has always been a person that will come around after the fact and things have blown over so she can act like she was there the entire time.

Everything the little boy needed, Tamara and her mother provided for him. Now Tamara was getting some financial assistance for taking care of the little boy but not a lot so whatever that check didn't cover, Tamara and her mother covered it.

Tamara later realized that not only did that little boy need her but she needed that little boy too. Shemika knew her best friend had that problem that she wouldn't be able to bear children and because she knew she wasn't ready to be a mother and be a good mother, she allowed her friend Tamara to raise her son and love him like he should be loved and she gave him everything and she promised herself and the little boy that she was going to be the best mother that she could be.

Now this little boy isn't so little anymore but he needed to know the truth because she didn't want him finding out some other kind of way and being upset with his mother for not telling him," I said.

"Mom, that story is about us huh? So you're not my biological mother?" Calvin asked. "No, I'm not baby. I went through the paperwork and training to become your foster mother to now your adopted mother. Son, I'm sorry for just now telling you but I felt like you were way too young for me to tell you then but I didn't want you ever growing up, thinking that something was wrong with you for the reason why Shemika didn't want you because that's not the reason," I said.

"So what was the reason why she didn't keep me and raise me on her own?" Calvin asked. "Calvin, Shemika didn't know how to raise anyone because she never felt love growing up herself from her family. Sometimes when a person wasn't raised up in a family with love, they feel how can they show love to another human being, when they never had it themselves?

You can't ask someone to give someone something that they never had before. If I ask you for a billion dollars, you're going to look at me crazy, like where am I going to get a billion dollars from. See son, I can't expect that from you if you never had it before to give me.

Son, your biological mother's name is Shemika Ellison. I haven't seen or talked to her since that day she asked me to watch you that night with her boyfriend. I'm sure Shemika and that guy aren't together anymore and I wouldn't be surprised if Shemika isn't on drugs or locked up somewhere. So Calvin, the best thing that your mother could've done was given you to me and my mother to raise you.

I don't approve with how she did it by just leaving you and not telling me the truth but I understood why she did it. I just wanted you to know that just because I'm not your biological mother, I'm your mother in every shape and form of the word mother. I just didn't birth you, that's all," I said.

Calvin stood up from beside me on his bed and hugged me tightly. "Mom, thank you for telling me the truth. It means a lot to me but to be honest with you, I already knew the entire story," Calvin said. "Huh? How?" I asked.

"Grandma told me when I was about ten years old. She made me promise that I would never tell you that I knew the story until you were ready to tell me yourself and I didn't. As far as I'm concerned, you're my mother and always will be my mother," Calvin said. "Thank you baby. I feel the same exact way too. Now you get ready for bed. You have to go get those millions of dollars," I said.

As I held on to my son in our embrace, I felt something was about to happen that was going to drag my family through something. The devil knows how to try you when things are going your way but "whatever you got for me devil, trust me, I have God on my side and I'll be ready. No matter what it is."

Chapter 27

Get Out

I JUST GOT HOME FROM WORK and was feeling a little tired. I'm so glad that Calvin got his driver's license last week, so now he drives Mom's car to and from school. I gave Calvin the third degree and told him if he doesn't follow the rules or is on his phone, then I would take that car back from him so fast and sell it. He told me I won't have to worry about that because he's going to do the right thing.

Calvin even started dating someone at school. The young lady's name is Tina and she's a cheerleader and plays basketball as well. Calvin says Tina is an "A" honor roll student as well and just as smart as he is. I told him to be careful with Tina because he's some young lady's dream and especially what he's trying to do with his life. He told me he would be.

I wanted to talk to Calvin about sex and that if he's going to do that he needs to protect himself. I told him not to fall for "I'm on the pill," nonsense because that's a lie to try and get what they want. His mother

Shemika knew how to play that game a little too well but it never worked out for her.

Shemika thought she was going to trick Calvin's father into doing that but what Calvin's father did is hired two manly looking females to go and teach Shemika a lesson. Shemika looked like she was hit by a train and she stayed in the hospital for almost two weeks, from recovering from the beat down those ladies gave her. She had two broken ribs, a broken leg and a broken arm and one of the ladies gave her five-thousand dollars after they whipped her behind and told her not to ever contact Mr. Big again.

That's what she called him then. I tried to tell Shemika that her Mr. Big seemed dangerous and she better be careful but of course that went through one ear and out the other one. I told Calvin all about the situation about how I adopted and raised him, last night. I think I did a good job not bashing Shemika for how she just left Calvin on me, like he was some stray dog and she was tired of dealing with him.

I had no idea that Mom had already told Calvin and told him not to say anything to me, until I said something to him. I guess Mom didn't want it to be too much on me trying to tell him on my own. I'm glad he's not the typical, hardheaded young man that stays all under his friends and tries to do everything they're out there doing.

Calvin is more the type that will speak and talk to anyone. I remember one day when Calvin and

I were in the grocery store and this young lady was waiting with her mom but Calvin didn't see her. When Calvin passed her and she noticed it was Calvin, she said "Mom, that's my friend Calvin," The young lady was special needs with down syndrome. Calvin turned around when he saw the young lady and he hugged her and kissed her on the cheek. Calvin told her it was good to see her and he hugged her mother as well.

I asked Calvin about the young lady and he said her name is Kayla and the kids use to pick at her and make fun of her and he and his best friend Trevor, started sitting with Kayla at lunch and everyone stopped picking at her and about two, three weeks later, everyone started sitting beside Kayla at school. He told me they knew not to bother her when him and Trevor were around.

Kayla's mother waved me down one day and told me that she knew I had to be proud of my son because he is definitely one of a kind. She told me how Calvin and Trevor love Kayla, and protect her like they're her two big brothers. The mother told me that Kayla said that Calvin even snatched someone up for bothering her one day and Calvin told the guy he better not ever bother Kayla again.

The woman told me that she knows I'm proud of the young man that I'm raising because he is definitely an extraordinary young man. I walked away from the lady in tears. I didn't have instructions on how to be a mother but Mom told me she would help me as long as

I was serious about doing it and she did. To know my son has a heart of gold is the best feeling in the world and it ensured me that I must be doing something right as his mother.

I finally snapped out of going down memory lane, thinking of all the fond memories I had raising Calvin. Dammon told me he was going to bring dinner over tonight, that way I wouldn't have to cook anything. Calvin said that Dammon has been talking a lot about signing on with the Boston Celtics and that it would be in his best interest. I told Calvin to wait and see and not to jump with the first NBA team that showed a little interest in him, because he could definitely get a better offer if he just waited it out a little.

Calvin did that and so far he's had four other NBA teams that left messages for him and two other ones from last week. I told him to keep listening to his mother because I definitely wasn't going to steer him in the wrong direction.

Dammon said he's coming over around six-thirty so I told Calvin to be home by then and he assured me he would be. I started tidying up the house a little to make sure the house wasn't in bad shape or anything. I jumped in the shower and put on something a little more comfortable.

I was doing better at functioning through life without Mom and seeing Mrs. Ollie Mae's face at work but I was doing okay for the most part. I think keeping up with Calvin's meetings with the NBA, coaches, and college scouts is a full schedule and it's definitely not for the weak.

Dammon brought Chinese over and we all sat in the kitchen and ate. Dammon kept talking about how good of an offer Mr. Marrow made for playing with the Celtics. "Dammon, you don't think we should wait to see if we have other options on the table? I don't think that Calvin should just jump at the first offer that was thrown at him," I said. "To be honest, this might be the best one he gets," Dammon said. "Okay, we will definitely keep that in mind," I said.

I could see the disappointment in Dammon's eyes, as if that was the last thing he wanted to hear. "Calvin already has five offers from other NBA teams. He got an offer from the Lakers, the Heat, Phoenix Suns, the Mavericks, and the Spurs, so he is doing good and all of them are willing to pay more as a sign-on bonus and an impressive first year contract," I said.

Dammon looked like he was about to get sick. I grabbed my phone and placed it in the dining room chair. "Calvin, can you help me put something in the garage please. Dammon, Calvin and I will be back," I said. "Oh take your time, I need to make a phone call anyway," Dammon said.

Calvin followed me outside towards my car. "Mom, what do you need me to help you put in the garage?" Calvin asked. "Sweetheart, I don't have anything. I want to see if we can trust Dammon. I think that Mr. Marrow offered Dammon a few million dollars to try to get you to sign on with the Boston Celtics and that's why he is pressuring you so hard. Dammon is only trying to use you baby," I said.

"Mom you think so? I don't think he will do that?" Calvin said. I swear I love my son but he is so naïve to certain things. "Okay Calvin, I'm going to prove it to you. Dammon said he had to make a phone call right? Let's see how quick he's going to get off the phone when we come back inside and plus I have something set up, to see if he is actually genuine with trying to help you, or just looking out for himself," I said. "How you gonna do that Mom?" Calvin asked. "You'll see son," I said.

Calvin and I walked back inside and as soon as we walked back in the kitchen, Dammon got off the phone quickly. I took my phone from my chair and walked inside my bedroom. I mashed the play button on my phone to hear all of Dammon's conversation, when we walked out of the dining room. "Hey Mr. Marrow, it's me Dammon, I wanted you to know that I'm talking to my girlfriend and Calvin about trying to get him to sign on with the Boston Celtics but I want to know if you're willing to offer him a little more? He has several NBA teams that's trying to get him to sign with them. Will you be willing to pay fifteen million and five million dollars to me, and offer him twenty-five million for his first year? If you can do that, then I'm confident I can probably bring him along," Dammon said.

I shook my head at what I just heard Dammon say but then again, I figured he was all about the money he thought he was entitled to by getting Calvin on with the Celtics. I walked back in the kitchen and sat back at the kitchen table, while Dammon still was going on and on about Calvin playing for the Celtics. I decided to burst his bubble, and expose him for the snake he actually is.

"Tell me Dammon, what's in it for you if Calvin signs on with the Celtics?" I asked. "Nothing. I just want to see Calvin making all those Benjamins that I know he can be making by playing for them. God is going to bless me down the line," Dammon said.

I just shook my head, not being able to take any more of his lies. I pressed play on my phone and turned the volume up so he and Calvin could hear the recording. Dammon's mouth dropped and so did Calvin's when he heard what Dammon was trying to negotiate his life with Mr. Marrow. Dammon wasn't concerned about Calvin's future, all he wanted was those few millions that Mr. Marrow was going to throw his way. When the recorder had ended, I just stared at him, and shook my head.

"Dammon, I think it's best that you don't work with Calvin anymore. Calvin needs somebody who has his back and is not just looking to sign him just so they could make a profit off him like he's some piece of property or something. Take care and please don't call or come by here again," I said.

Dammon got up slowly, still looking at me, like he had something to say but he didn't say anything. He grabbed the doorknob and then looked back. "I'm sorry Tamara. I saw all those dollar signs and I got a little greedy and selfish and just started thinking about myself and not what's best for Calvin. Please forgive me," Dammon said. "Okay, thank you for admitting that but I think we're both good," I said, getting up and walking towards the door.

Dammon left and I closed and locked the door behind him and walked back over to the table. "Mom, we don't need him. It's just you and me, like it's always been," Calvin said. "That's right baby, but at this time, and at my age, I just wish that Dammon was an actual keeper but I guess he's not," I said. "I guess not Mom, but you'll find someone one day and I have a feeling it will be soon," Calvin said.

Chapter 28

Arrested

JUST FINISHED MY ROUNDS AT work and was preparing to go on my lunch break. As I walked by Mrs. Ollie Mae's room, I noticed an older black woman putting her things in the dresser drawers. "Hello. How are you?" I asked, saying hello as I walked in the woman's room. The lady turned around and walked towards me and started pushing me out of her room. "Out. Get out of my room. Don't you see me trying to get settled?" the woman said, closing the door in my face. "I guess she doesn't like no one in her room?" I said to myself.

"I guess she told you huh?" Pam said, laughing. "You saw that?" I asked. "I sure did. Maybe she doesn't warm up to people as easy as Mrs. Ollie Mae did," Pam said. "Maybe not but if she doesn't want to interact with me then I won't. The last thing I'm going to do is force myself on her," I said. "Well, I'm sure she'll warm up to you soon," Pam said.

I was about to walk off when Pam stopped me. "Tamara, I wanted to say congratulations to your son for getting the highest score in that game. I know you're extremely proud of him aren't you?" Pam said. "I certainly am. I couldn't tell you how much I'm thankful to God for allowing my son to use all his talent, which is definitely paying off for him.

I went in the break room and warmed up my lunch. I had a little Chinese food left from when Dammon brought over for dinner last night. I really regret how things turned out between us. I wouldn't say it surprised me because people will do all kinds of things when they think money is on the line.

I finished my lunch and threw my things in the trash. I was heading back to the nurse's station, when I saw two police officers, coming from Pam's office. "Lord, what in the world has Pam has done to have the police coming to the job for?" I said to myself.

Pam and the officers started walking my direction. "Tamara, these officers need to see you?" Pam, said. "How can I help you?" I asked, wondering why the police were here to see me. "Are you Tamara Martin Williams?" one of the officers asked. "Yes, I am," I said. "Ma'am, you have the right to remain silent. Anything you say can be held against you in the court of law. You have the right to an attorney," the officer said, as he continued reading me my rights.

At first I thought I was having a terrible nightmare or something, because this can't be happening in real life. I needed someone to slap me to make sure I'm not asleep. Pam came towards me, where the officers were standing. "Officers, this must be some kind of mistake. Whatever you think this woman did can't be true. You're making a huge mistake," Pam said.

"Officer, what am I being charged with?" I asked. "Kidnapping," the officer said. "Kidnapping!" I yelled. "Yes, you took someone's child sixteen years ago," the officer said, taking me out of the building. When the officer said kidnapping, my heart nearly stopped. This had Shemika's name all over it. This chick set all this up and had the police coming after me after she dumped Calvin off on me.

"Tamara, is there anyone you need me to call for you?" Pam asked. "Yes. Call my son and tell him to look in my middle dresser drawer and look on that orange piece of paper that's folded up, and call Mr. Lawrence Collins. Tell him to tell Mr. Collins that I'm a friend of Mrs. Ollie Mae and she told me if I ever got into trouble, to call him," I said. "Okay, I'm on it now," Pam said. "Thank you Pam," I replied. "No problem. I'm sure they will get everything straight," Pam said. "I sure hope so," I replied.

The police pulled off and it suddenly hit me that I was definitely on my way to jail and there was nothing I could do about it. We arrived at the police department and they stripped me down and made me put on that God awful orange jumpsuit. I looked like I belong on "Orange is the New Black," or something and I was screaming, "I'm innocent! I didn't do anything! I'm innocent!"

They took my mugshots and fingerprinted me to complete the process. They put me in a single jail cell and when they closed the door behind me, I knew this was it. There wasn't a camera crew that jumped out to say "ma'am, you've been punk'd," or anything like that. I was actually in a real jail and all this was really happening to me.

I laid down on this disgusting mattress, not wanting to even think about all the stains that were all over this thing. I would feel a little more comfortable if I had a can of Raid to spray this entire thing from front to back, three or four times, and then I might be able to sleep on it.

This is crazy that I'm in here for something that I didn't do. God spoke to me and told me "weep in May, endure for the night but joy cometh in the morning." I'm not quite sure what God is trying to tell me. Was he telling me that everything would be alright in the morning?

I need answers and I needed them now. I'm sitting here, praying and wondering what I did to have this happening to me right now. "Guard! Guard!" I yelled. "Yes!" A woman guard came towards me. "What is it that you want ma'am?" the guard asked. "May I have my first phone call please?" I asked. "Sure," the officer said, walking with me to a phone booth. "You have ten minutes," the officer said, as she walked away and closed the door behind her.

I quickly called Calvin. "Mom, why are you in jail? I was shocked when Ms. Pam called me and told me that," Calvin said. "They said I kidnapped you, but that isn't true," I said. "Mom, please tell me you didn't do that?" Calvin asked. "No I didn't. I would never take a child from their mother," I said.

Calvin was quiet on the phone and not saying anything, like he didn't believe me. "Did you call the number that I asked you to call?" I asked. "Yes. The man said he would be there first thing in the morning," Calvin said. "What's his name?" I asked. "His name is Lawrence Collins," Calvin said. "Calvin, you did tell him that Mrs. Ollie Mae gave me his number right?" I asked. "Yes I did," Calvin said, sounding like he had attitude.

"Calvin, is something wrong? Why are you acting like that?" I asked. "Because you're charged with kidnapping me. Mom, please tell me you didn't kidnapped me from my parents? You didn't take me from them did you?" Calvin asked.

I swear if Calvin was in front of me and asked me that stupid question, I might have knocked some sense into him. "Of course not. Like I just told you a few minutes ago, I would never take a child from his mother. Calvin I can't believe you would even say something like that to me. You think if I had kidnapped you, I would stay in Manning and raise you? Do you know how small Manning is and how these people would be talking? Calvin look, I can't stop you for believing what you choose to believe but I'm done explaining myself to you," I said.

"Mom, I don't know what to believe," Calvin said. "Look, I don't have any more time left to talk," I said. "Okay Mom," Calvin said. "You have a goodnight son and keep me in your prayers. I love you Calvin," I said. "Thanks," Calvin said, hanging up the phone.

I stood there holding the phone in my hands with tears. My son didn't even say he loved me back. I guess he thinks that I'm really capable of kidnapping a child and taking them from their mother. "God please let the truth be revealed so I can clear my name," Amen.

Chapter 29

Lawrence Collins

I WAS FINALLY ABLE TO FALL asleep in my cell last night. I can't believe that I spent the night in this dungeon. It's not actually as bad as it seems on TV but it's still not a piece of cake either, or a place I'm trying to get used to. I sat in my cell, staring at the wall as if these walls would eventually talk to me and ask me how I ended up in a place like this.

I know Shemika is behind this but why? Why would she do me like this and I took her son in when no one else would. When I asked her mother Ms. Sarah and she told me flat out no and then I asked Abbigail and she told me the same thing. I wonder if they know what Shemika is up to and will they speak on my behalf, if this goes to court.

My mind was all over the place and I had no idea what I'm going to do. If my mother was alive she would move heaven and hell to make sure I was home, if not last night at least today. My mother wasn't going to let her baby rot in jail for nobody.

I saw the female guard come and hit on my cell. "Ma'am, your attorney Mr. Collins is here to see you," the officer said, opening my cell door. I followed her into a small room. "Hello ma'am, I'm Lawrence Collins. I understand you knew my Aunt Ollie Mae," Mr. Collins said. "Yes. I was your aunt's nurse before she died," I said. "Okay. I guess my aunt knew you would be needing me, before she died. My aunt had the gift of seeing and knowing things before they actually happened. My mom said, that was just a gift my aunt always had, even when they were children," Mr. Collins said.

"I swear that woman knew she could see things that no one else could," I said. "She certainly could. I remember growing up, she would tell us not to do something while we were about to do it. I thought the woman had eyes in the back of her head or something," Mr. Collins said, laughing.

Mr. Collins sat down at the table across from me. "Ms. Martin, you do know that you're being charged for kidnapping right?" Mr. Collins said. "Yes, I know. But Mr. Collins, I didn't kidnap anyone," I said. "Ms. Martin, I need you to tell me your story because I need to know what happened so I can defend you," Mr. Collins said. "Well, my best friend Shemika and her boyfriend Greg came to my mother's house Friday night and asked me to babysit her son, which is my godson, Calvin. I told her I would. Shemika told me that she would be back in about three hours when the movie was over but she never came to get Calvin.

I haven't laid eyes on my so called best friend, since the day she dropped her son off at my house. Now I had to go to work the next night, so I went over to talk to Ms. Sarah and Abbigail, Shemika's mother and sister. They both told me that they didn't hear anything from Shemika and I asked if they could take Calvin in and they both said no. They both suggested that I call the police and Child Protective Services.

I called the police and got in touch with Child Protective Services and they granted me to be Calvin's foster mother, until they could find someone to take him in or adopt him. Mr. Lawrence, things haven't been easy for me being a single woman but my mother helped me raise Calvin.

I later got married but things didn't work out in my marriage and I moved back in with my mother to help me with Calvin," I said. "So, you went through all the court hearings to adopt your son and what about your best friend's mother and sister, were they supportive with you adopting Calvin?" Mr. Lawrence asked. "Yes they were. Just as long as they didn't have to raise him themselves," I said.

"I'm so sorry your dealing with this but since you went through the court system and properly filed your adoption, it should be easy to get you out on bond, until your trial day," Lawrence said. "Okay," I replied. "Give me about an hour and I'll come back to get you out on bond. I'm not one-hundred percent they will grant me bond but I'm sure I can.

I stood up and shook Mr. Lawrence's hand. "Thank you Mr. Lawrence for whatever you can do," I said. "You're welcome but don't thank me yet, until I can get you off. I do have one last question though," Mr. Lawrence said.

"What's that?" I asked. "Why do you think your best friend is accusing you of kidnapping her son?" Mr. Lawrence asked. "Mr. Lawrence, my son is Calvin Martin? Have you heard of him?" I asked. "Yes, I'm not sure from where though but I definitely have heard that name before," Mr. Lawrence said.

"Mr. Lawrence, my son is Manning's basketball rising star Calvin Martin, and he has offers to be drafted straight into the NBA after high school. Shemika and her family are money hungry and she's seeing dollar signs all over this case she created," I said. "Horrible. She'll get exactly what she deserves," Mr. Lawrence said.

I stood up and shook Mr. Lawrence's hand. "Thank you Mr. Lawrence for whatever you can do," I replied. "You're welcome, but again don't thank me yet," Mr. Lawrence said. "Okay," I replied.

The female officer escorted me back to my cell. "Ma'am," I called out. "Yes," the officer replied. "Why am I going through this? This was supposed to be my best friend that asked me to watch her son over sixteen years ago and now she comes from wherever she's been hiding and accusing me of kidnapping her son. Now if I kidnapped her son, what sense does it make to continue staying in my mother's house with supposedly her son that I kidnapped?

Why would I stay here and not move out the state or something? Why would I stay in little Manning, South Carolina, where everyone knows everyone's business? Does that make any sense to you?" I asked. "No it doesn't. Do you have any idea why she's doing this to you?" the officer asked. "Yes, because she sees my son as a jackpot, now since he's about to go in the NBA, so she's trying to paint the picture that I stole her child from her. If Calvin just grew up as a normal young man, maybe working at a factory job or something, I would've never heard from her," I said.

"Well, if your friend is doing this for a cash out, trust me, it will all come out one way or the other. God has a way of exposing people for who and what they are and she'll definitely get hers," the officer said, as she opened my cell to let me inside.

I walked inside my cell and got down on my knees to pray.

"Dear God,

Whatever Shemika is up to, let it be revealed in court. Allow her to get all this back that she's trying to put on me. I have a feeling God that you're about to reveal everything that's been hidden

and allow it to come to the light. Thank
you Lord for everything, Amen."

I got up off the floor and sat back on the bed and
then closed my eyes to reflect on everything that's
going on around me. "Mom, I can't take all this. I'm
not cut out for this kind of thing. Jail is definitely not
for the weak but I won't pretend to be strong because
it's taking a toll on me and I don't know how much
longer I can take this."

I finally realized exactly what Mrs. Ollie Mae was
trying to tell me that day in her room. There was going
to be something that was going to happen to me that
was going to turn my life upside down but to be patient
and just wait on God and it will all eventually come
out. That's exactly what I have to do is just wait on
God.

Chapter 30

Trust No One

LAWRENCE HAS BEEN WORKING ON my case and coming by to see me, to give me details. The judge denied me bail due to the severity of my charge. I guess out of fear that I'll skip town or something. I told Lawrence I don't know how much longer I can take being locked up in a place like this, like I'm some kind of wild animal or something. The walls look like they were actually closing in on me. It's been three months since I've been here.

I wonder if Lawrence is actually working on my case, like he says he is. The more I sit here and think, the more my mind was taking me to a dark place of depression and I was trying my best not to go there, but this jail cell will have you thinking all kinds of things.

I've been praying, reading my Bible, along with other books and exercising as often as I can to keep my mind focused and to stay away from the darkness that I was heading down to.

There are four other inmates in here. They seem friendly but this isn't a place that I'm trying to be friends with anyone, like we'll be calling each other or having lunch or something. When I get out of this place, I'm never looking back or trying to talk to anyone that's affiliated with this place.

I haven't heard from Calvin at all. I told him we can have visitors from ten-o'clock on Sunday mornings to two-o'clock that afternoon, but he hasn't tried to come see me. I think he actually thinks that I kidnapped him and took him away from his birth mother. Lawrence asked me about him and as soon as he brought his name up, I started crying.

I gave up my entire young life raising him. I had to deny myself things that I wanted to make sure he had and this is the thanks I get. I can understand Calvin being a little skeptical but I told him I didn't do what I'm being accused of, but I could hear the skepticism in his voice, like he wasn't sure if I wasn't telling the truth or not.

I sat in the activity room, watching whatever was on TV. I just needed a distraction and the TV was definitely doing that. Lisa, one of the inmates came and sat beside me. "Hello Tamara. How are you doing today?" Lisa asked. "I'll be better once I get up out of here," I said. "You and I both," Lisa replied.

Lisa seems to be okay but she seems a little too clingy and I'm not sure about her. "Tamara, what are you in here for?" Lisa asked. "I stole some items from the grocery store and I got caught," I said. "How much did you steal?" Lisa asked. "About one hundred dollars' worth of stuff," I said, knowing I was lying. I wasn't about to tell this woman why I'm in here, like that's any of her business. For all I know this could be some kind of set up. "I guess you and your family were hungry huh?" Lisa said, smiling. "I guess so," I replied.

"What about you?" I asked. "Well, I went out riding with my boyfriend in his brand new Camaro for a few days. The only thing about that is the fool never told me that his brand new Camaro was stolen. So I'm out on the passenger side relaxing, while the wind is blowing through my hair. Girl you should've seen me, smiling away until I saw those blue lights shining behind us with all those sirens as well.

There was only one police car behind us and before I knew it, there were like ten behind us, in a matter of no time. I looked at my boyfriend, and he had a crazy behind look on his face, and Tamara, I just knew that fool had done something that he wasn't telling me. I asked him what did he do and he told me that he stole the car. Girl, I felt the devil come out of me, and I turned around and slapped him so freaking hard, while he was driving, I thought sure he was going to run straight up into a brick wall.

My boyfriend decided he could out run the cops since he was in a faster car. He was all over the place so instead of me getting pissed off with him, there was no need to, since I knew I was going to jail too. So I kicked back and enjoyed the ride as well," Lisa said, smiling. "What kind of car was it again?" I asked. "It was a candy apple red Camaro," Lisa said. "Oh okay," I replied. "Do you have any kids?" I asked. "Yes, I have three. What about you?" Lisa asked. "No kids," I said. "No kids. Okay," Lisa said. I couldn't help notice the way Lisa looked at me, as if she had a lot more to say but didn't. "What do you do for a living?" Lisa asked. "Lisa, I don't mind us talking but please no personal questions," I said. "Oh, I'm sorry," Lisa replied.

There was something about Lisa that I didn't trust, even though this was our first real conversation but I couldn't help that feeling that there's a story behind her and I definitely don't want to find out.

Lisa went back to her bunk but every now and then I caught her looking at me. I sure hope Lisa doesn't think that when the lights go out, she'll be trying to pull the covers off me, because I'll beat Lisa down in this jail cell, if she tried something like that.

I know my day is coming that I'll soon be released and get out of here and I certainly can't wait. This is definitely not a place for me. I couldn't imagine how people could be locked up in a place like this the majority of their lives and once they get out, they do something crazy and get locked up again to end up right back in a place like that. I guess being in a place like this for so long, that's what you get accustomed to and feel like you can't survive without it. I hope I'll never get used to this place.

Chapter 31

My Trial Begins

L AWRENCE CAME BY TO TALK to me last week and he asked if there was anyone to corroborate my story about Shemika and Greg coming by my house to ask me to watch Calvin. I told Lawrence that my mother was dead and the only other person was Greg, wherever he's at. I also told Lawrence that the next morning I went by Ms. Sarah's house as well and Abbigail's job to talk with her.

I told Lawrence that Ms. Sarah's nosey neighbors were also outside and listening to every word I said to her, they were only about a few feet away from us. The two old ladies heard everything and they even commented to me about how nasty Ms. Sarah was for not taking in her own grandchild. Lawrence asked if I had any evidence that Abbigail and Ms. Sarah knew that I had Calvin and I told him I do. I had pictures at birthday parties that Abbigail's children had, with Calvin in the pictures next to his cousins and his grandmother Ms. Sarah. Abbigail was also in the pictures.

Lawrence asked where the pictures were stored and I told him in a little red box on the top of my dresser. That's where I keep all my pictures. I told Lawrence that Calvin would give him the box.

I don't know if Lawrence ever found the pictures, since I haven't talked to him since he came by last week. I just know that the lady officer told me that I needed to be dressed and ready this morning for my trial. I sat on the edge of my bed, waiting for them to transport me to my trial hearing. I walked inside with Lawrence and took my seat inside court. The prosecutor is a tall dark-skinned man. I've heard his name before, Timothy Sylvester.

I knew Timothy's face from somewhere but couldn't remember where or how I knew him. After Timothy's opening statement, I knew exactly where I knew him from. Timothy and I went to school together but he graduated two years ahead of me. Timothy actually had a crush on Shemika. I don't think they ever went out or anything but I'm sure Shemika did some other things with him.

Timothy had a good opening statement but he's trying to put me in prison for something I didn't do. I tried making eye contact with Shemika but of course she wouldn't look next my way, after all she's done. I can see why.

Lawrence stood up to give his opening statement. I sure hope Lawrence knows what he's doing because I can't go to prison for something I didn't do. I guess I'm about to see just what kind of lawyer he really is.

"Ladies and gentlemen of the court and this fine jury, I have no idea why we're here. I don't know if my client even knows why she's here. My client was asked sixteen years ago by supposedly her best friend and her boyfriend to watch her son until they went to the movies and she was supposed to come back to get her son, three hours later but she never came back.

Now the person that's accusing my client is supposed to be her best friend, but what kind of best friend asks her best friend to watch her son, her responsibility, so she and her boyfriend could go out, but instead of her just going out, she never came back. She never called her friend or anything, to tell her nothing.

She threw her son off on her best friend to raise him. Why would she do that, and never come back? This supposed mother wanted to live her own life. She didn't want to be tied down by a child, a little boy or a responsibility. She threw her son away and didn't look back not even one time, but I promise you, I know the reason why she waited now out of all this time to come forth and send her best friend to prison.

But by the time this trial is over with, you'll see exactly who deserves to go to prison for wasting this court's time and snatching three months of this young lady's life away from her and away from her job and son. Thank you," Lawrence said, as he took his seat.

"Mr. Sylvester, you may call your first witness please," the judge said. "Your Honor, I call Ms. Sarah Miller to the stand," Timothy said. Sarah walked up front and put her hand on the Bible as the bailiff swore her in.

"Ms. Sarah, when was the last time you saw your daughter?" Timothy asked. "It's been a few years ago," Ms. Sarah said. "About how long is a few years ago?" Timothy asked. "About five years ago," Ms. Sarah said, which I knew was a lie. "Did your daughter ask you if you knew where her son was living or where he was at?" Timothy asked. "Yes. I told her I didn't know," Sarah said. "Well did you know where your grandson was living?" Ms. Sarah asked. "No, I didn't," Ms. Sarah said.

I wanted to stand up and tell Ms. Sarah she was lying but I knew I had to control myself, before I got thrown out of the courtroom. Timothy asked Ms. Sarah a few more questions before he took his seat. Lawrence stood up to walk towards the stand.

"So Ms. Sarah, from my understanding, you're telling us all that you didn't know that Tamara had Calvin living with her?" Lawrence asked. "No, I didn't," Ms. Sarah said. "Ms. Sarah, you do know that telling a lie or lying is considered perjury while under oath right? That means you can be charged and locked up if we can prove that you're lying," Lawrence said. "I know," Ms. Sarah said, still not changing her story.

"Ms. Sarah, so Ms. Tamara didn't come to your place the next day, asking you if you've seen Shemika and if you could take your grandson because she had to go to work that night?" Lawrence asked. "No she didn't," Ms. Sarah said. "Ms. Sarah, do you recognize these two people? Could you both stand up and raise your hands, Ms. Mattie and Mrs. Ida?" Lawrence asked as the two women raised their hands and stood up.

"Ms. Sarah, these two ladies were at the front porch which is only a few feet away from your door and they will testify to hearing your conversation with Tamara, as she asked you if you knew where your daughter was and if you would take your grandson in. You told Tamara no and they are willing to testify on what they heard and what they saw. Ms. Sarah, I also have pictures of you at your grandchildren's birthday parties with you hugging and sitting around all your grandchildren. So you might want to think about your entire testimony today because I already caught you in a lie once, don't dig yourself deeper and deeper, until you're in a hole that you can't get yourself out of," Lawrence said.

Lawrence had Ms. Sarah exactly where he wanted her. She had no other choice but to tell the truth, but she didn't say anything further. "Ms. Sarah, we all know the truth that you were fully aware of what was going on and you pretending like you didn't is only a lie. I'm going to stop asking you any more questions because I don't want you to get in any more trouble than you're in already," Lawrence said.

Ms. Sarah stepped down and then Lawrence called his next witness which was Abbigail. Abbigail told the truth and said how Shemika did exactly what she wanted to do and has always done and always left the people she's supposed to love to clean up her mess. She said this time she left her one-year-old son behind for her best friend to raise.

Lawrence asked a few more questions and then he sat down. I think he was painting the jury a pretty good picture of who Shemika is and who she's always been. I hope by the time all this is over with, she will realize that she just can't do anything she wants to people and expect them to take up the slack. This time Shemika has to be held accountable for everything.

Chapter 32

Husband!

THIS TRIAL WAS TAKING A lot out of me and I wish I could go home and just lie down in my own bed, and away from everyone. I can't believe how Ms. Sarah just sat up there and just lied like that, but Mom always said that Shemika was just like her mother and she was definitely right. Ms. Sarah didn't care about helping anyone and neither did Shemika. I can't believe this girl has me up in court for something she knows dang well I didn't do or ask for. I sure hope she burns in hell for everything she's doing to me, as well as Ms. Sarah, for going along with her.

"Mr. Sylvester, please call your next witness," the judge said. "I call my client's husband to the stand, Mr. Steven Williams," Timothy said. My mouth dropped and I know my heartbeat had to have missed a few beats. I know I had to be losing it, to hear Timothy call out my ex-husbands name. Steven walked up front and placed his hand on the Bible, while the bailiff sworn him in.

I was just looking, waiting for a camera crew to jump out of anywhere and scream, "Tamara Martin, you just got punk'd," and everyone start falling over laughing. There is no way in the world that Steven and Shemika are married. Did Shemika go out looking for Steven or did Steven go out there looking for her? Steven definitely knew all about Shemika because I explained it to him when we first started dating. Did he do this to hurt me? Some kind of sick revenge or something, he's trying to take out on me?

"Mr. Williams, how long have you been married to my client?" Timothy asked. "Eight beautiful years," Steven said. "Okay nice, but don't you have history with Ms. Tamara Martin as well?" Timothy asked. "Yes. Tamara is my ex-wife," Steven said. "How long have you and Tamara been married?" Timothy asked. "We were married for a few months until we got our divorce," Steven said. "Why did you two get a divorce?" Timothy asked. "I guess we were a little too young," Steven said.

I couldn't help it, I burst out laughing. Lawrence quickly popped at my hand, letting me know that wasn't cool, while the judge gave me a chastising look. I had to compose myself before I end up getting kicked out of court. "Mr. Williams, did you know anything about when your ex-wife had kidnapped my client's son?" Timothy asked. "I object your Honor. Mr. Sylvester doesn't know whether or not my client kidnapped anyone," Lawrence said. "Sustain, Mr. Sylvester. Don't do that again," the judge stated.

"I'm sorry your Honor," Timothy said. "Well Mr. Williams, did you know that your ex-wife Tamara, was raising your wife's son?" Timothy asked. "No I didn't know that. I thought Tamara had given birth to Calvin and she was his biological mother. I had no idea that she didn't. She always acted so nervous when people were around, as if she didn't want anyone to get close to him, as if she was afraid they would ask him some kind of questions or something," Steven said, lying through his teeth.

I would say I'm surprised that Steven would lie like that in a courtroom but then again, I'm not. Steven was fully aware that Calvin was adopted and that his mother and I were best friends, but then again, he wants to paint that picture that I kidnapped my son. He wants to make me look like a villain. As if I just snatched Calvin away from Shemika, while she was cooking dinner or out of his bed or something.

Timothy finally sat down and Lawrence was questioning Steven now. "Steven, I read your file and what led to your divorce? And it says that you have a terrible temper, along with mental illness as well right?" Lawrence asked. "Your Honor, I object. The witness isn't up to discuss his mental state," Timothy said. "Well your Honor, he wanted him to talk about his first marriage to my client, which involves his mental illness, which led to their divorce, so Mr. Sylvester opened that door," Lawrence said. "That's right Mr. Sylvester, you did open that door, so I'm going to allow it. Please answer the question Mr. Williams," the judge said.

"Yes. I suffer from mental illness which I take medication for now," Steven said. "Well, weren't you on medication back then as well, especially when you put your hands around Ms. Martin's neck and tried to choke her to death?" Lawrence asked. "I object your Honor. We aren't talking about something that happened over ten years ago, we're talking about this case right here," Timothy said. "You're right Mr. Sylvester, Mr. Collins, please move on and let's stay on this case and not bring up any other case that's is not of the present," the judge said.

Lawrence nodded his head. "So Steven, do you think that Tamara actually kidnapped Calvin from his biological mother, the one that you're now married to?" Lawrence asked. "Yes I do. I wouldn't put anything past Tamara," Steven said.

I shook my head at Steven's response, still trying to keep my composure. This fool tried to kill me and he's in this courtroom lying his behind off, trying to convince the judge and jury that I'm some monster that would take a child from their biological mother like that.

"God, I need a miracle right now. I need you to show yourself in this courtroom, and let the devil, know they will not win. God, you sit high and you look low, and I trust you. You said in your word, to have faith. We don't need a lot but just the size of a mustard seed and that's all I have, but right now my faith is being shaken and challenged by what Shemika is trying to do. Mom always told me, in Philippians 4:6, "Don't worry about anything; instead, pray about everything. Tell God what you need, and thank him for all he has done," and I'm thanking you God for what you're about to do, Amen."

Chapter 33

Shemika's Lies

STEVEN GOT OFF THE STAND and took a seat in the back of the courtroom. I wanted to get up and slap the taste out his mouth for sitting on that stand, lying through his teeth like that. Steven tried to drag me through the mud and then step all over me in the midst of it. How could I even love someone like him in the first place, but Eve said it best in her song, "Love is Blind, and it will take over your mind." That definitely had to be the case with Steven that his good looks and charm took over my mind and what I thought was love, was really only lust.

Timothy walked up to the stand, "I will like to call my client Shemika Miller Williams to the stand," Timothy said, as Shemika walked her little boney behind up to the stand. I swear I wanted to run up there behind her and drop kick her in the head. "Ma'am, do you swear to tell the truth, the whole truth and nothing but the truth, so help you God?" the bailiff asked. "Please, that thing wouldn't know what the truth is, if it was to fall on top of her head!" I yelled.

"Ma'am, I have been very lenient with you all day today with some of your outbursts and bursting out laughing. Now this is your last time doing that today or I will put you out of my courtroom. Do I make myself clear?" the judge asked. "Yes, your Honor and please forgive me," I said. "Very well, bailiff, you may continue swearing her in," the judge said.

I tried taking deep breaths to control my anger so I wouldn't have another outburst. "Tamara, I know this is frustrating for you but you have to control yourself. One more outburst like that, and the judge is going to throw you out of this courtroom and this trial will be for nothing. I promise you, I got this. Let me do my job and show you the type of lawyer that I am. Trust me, my aunt didn't steer you in the wrong direction," Lawrence said, with a reassuring smile.

I wanted so desperately to believe that Lawrence had this but this was my life, and not his life on the line here. If the jury finds me guilty, I could spend twenty to thirty years of my life in prison for a crime I didn't commit, now how fair is that? I looked back to see where Calvin was and he was sitting by some little girl, holding her hand. I guess that's his little Tina girlfriend he was telling me about before all this has happened.

I had to get back to the case and stay focused. I wanted to hear all the lies that Shemika was about to tell, because she was definitely going to milk this for all it's worth. "Mrs. Williams, do you mind telling me what happened that night that your son was kidnapped?" Timothy asked. "Well, I was at my apartment about to do laundry and Tamara was over at my house, looking after Calvin. I had a lot of laundry to do so I was gathering all my things together to go to the laundromat.

Tamara told me she was going outside to take Calvin to the playground to play. As I was putting my things in the car, Tamara came running and screaming, telling me she only turned her head for a second and when she turned around, she saw a man and a woman, grabbing Calvin, and throwing him inside a black car. This messed up my entire life. I was in and out of jail and living on the street, and addicted to drugs. I'm finally at a place that I'm okay and I've gotten myself together and now I'm here. I want my son back so I can be a mother to him now." Shemika said.

I just shook my head at all the BS Shemika was feeding these people. These women on the jury were actually rubbing their eyes, acting like they were crying, by the sob story that Shemika was telling them. If I didn't know any better, I would probably believe her too. She was just that convincing and she told that story with a straight face, that it would make me believe her if I didn't know any better.

"So Mrs. Williams, you coming by Tamara's house that Friday night with your boyfriend, asking her to watch your son, was a lie that Tamara made up? That wasn't true at all?" Timothy asked. "No, it wasn't. I don't know why Tamara would tell such horrible lies like that on me, saying that I abandoned my son and threw him off on her. That never happened. I love my son and I would never abandon him like that," Shemika said.

If I wasn't still under arrest, I would probably have to walk out of this courtroom, afraid of what I might do to this girl. This was someone that I called my best friend, my roll dawg, my ace, and my sister, only for her to make me out to be the bad guy in this situation, when all I did was tried to help her and keep Calvin with me so he wouldn't have to go to foster care, but that's the thanks I get.

Timothy finally sat down and Lawrence took the stand. "Mrs. Williams, I know you don't believe that story you just told this court, because guess what, I don't believe it. This young lady is not what you say she is, a kidnapper. You know that's not true. You do know that you have been sworn in and I promise you when the truth comes out, I am going to bring up all kinds of charges on you for what you took this young lady through.

This is someone that loves you enough to take your one-year-old son in and keep and raise him, so he wouldn't have to grow up in foster care. Your own mother didn't take him, nor your sister because they knew this is something you normally do. I'm telling you, you are in a world of trouble when the truth comes out. You had this young man, Calvin Martin not even wanting to see his mother while she was locked up, because he thought she actually kidnapped him," Lawrence said. "I'm his mother! Tamara, isn't his mother!" Shemika yelled.

"I can't tell. You dumped him off on her. You left him behind like a little stray dog, looking for someone to love him. Your friend did that. She loved this little boy and gave him a home and a family. She gave him stability and didn't have him running all over the place, from state to state or house to house. Ladies and gentleman, why in the world would someone kidnap a child, and tried to bring them to their mother and to their sister, so they could get him?

A kidnapper, would be far away in another state or on a low radar, afraid of being caught, but not Ms. Martin. Ms. Martin raised this young man in her mother's house, with her mother. She was a CNA at a nursing home, and she continued to go to school and graduated at the top of her class as a Registered Nurse. Why, because she wanted to give her son a good life. Mrs. Williams, a mother isn't just someone that births you and gives you life.

A mother is someone that wakes you up every morning, and helps you get ready for school. Someone that makes you breakfast and packs you your lunch to take to school. A mother is someone that helps you with your homework and tells you bedtime stories at night, when you can't fall asleep. A mother is someone that fixes you soup when you're sick and nurses you back to health so you'll feel better, and even takes days off at work to make sure there's someone there to take care of their child.

A mother, is the person that is at their sporting events, or there to see them get an award and jump up clapping and screaming, saying "that's my baby." That's a mother. So again, just because you gave birth to Calvin, doesn't by any means make you his mother and I think Calvin knows who his mother is and will always be.

Mrs. Williams, you should be ashamed of yourself for doing this to that young lady. Now I'm going to tell you what I'm going to do. I'm going to give you this last chance to admit to this court what you have done to this young lady. That you have lied and dragged this woman's name and reputation through the freaking mud, for nothing. You should be ashamed of yourself. Your mother, Ms. Sarah, should be ashamed of herself as well, for allowing this foolishness to go on and be a part of it as well.

Mrs. Williams, what's it going to be? Are you going to admit to the lies and betrayal you caused today in this court, with the false charges and allegations you have filed on Ms. Martin, or are you going to go ahead with this trial, because my next witness will blow this case up like an explosion if you force me to bring them in to testify," Lawrence replied. Shemika didn't say anything.

Lawrence signaled for someone to come in the courtroom. I turned around and I could've just slid out of my chair on the floor like a snake. Lord, behold it was Greg, Shemika's ex-boyfriend that came over to my house that Friday night, when she asked me to watch Calvin for her and never returned.

Shemika burst out crying because she knew her lies had finally come to an end and Lawrence had cracked the case wide open with the one person that could shed light on all of this and tell the truth. "Mrs. Williams, I'm going to give you one last chance to tell this court that you made all this up and that you don't want this to go on any further because once Mr. Greg Wilson takes this stand and tells his story of what happened that Friday night, as he remembers it, I can't help you beyond that point. You will be in the mercy of this court and I won't mind throwing you out to the wolves, as a piece of raw meat, for them to tear you alive, one by one. So you tell me what you want to do?"

"I'm sorry for everything. I lied about it all. Tamara never kidnapped Calvin from me. I didn't want her taking credit for my son's success when she couldn't have children of her own and Calvin came from me. I'm the one that gave birth to him and nursed him. I love you Calvin! I love you son!" Shemika shouted. "You may be the one that gave birth to him Mrs. Williams, but again a real mother is the one that raised him and that's not you. You gave up that right a long time ago and you forced someone else to do it. The only thing about that is, the person you forced it on, took joy in doing it and she gave that young man something he needed more than anything at the time, he needed a mother," Lawrence said.

Chapter 34

My Voice

THE JUDGE HIT HER GAVEL down to make her decision. "In light of this case, both lawyers have approached me that there is really no need to pursue any further charges on Ms. Tamara Martin so I'm going to dismiss all charges against Ms. Martin," the judge said. "Excuse me your Honor, I have something to say," I said. "Ma'am, there's really no need for you to say anything," the judge said. "Ma'am with all due respect but I was in jail, that God forsaken place for three months of my life, for something I didn't do, so I think I have a right to say what I have to say. I think I have suffered enough to at least have that granted to me," I said.

"You know what, you are absolutely right," the judge said. I walked up to the podium up front as the bailiff swore me in as I took a seat. "You know, I spent three months of my life in jail for something I didn't do. I was accused of kidnapping supposedly my best friend's child and she knew she lied through her teeth.

My so called best friend, who I've been friends with ever since I was five years old.

She came to my house that Friday night and asked me to watch her son because she and her boyfriend wanted to go to the movies and even though I didn't want to watch him, I did anyway. So I watched him but she was supposed to come back to get him after the movies were over, no later than three hours later.

I never knew that one particular night was going to change my life forever, because that was the last time I saw her and that was the night I became a mother. My so called best friend until today, I haven't seen her in sixteen years. She just left and never came back. Now mind you, I didn't have any children, so I didn't know one thing about being a mother to a child, I barely knew how to take care of myself, talking about a one-year-old little boy.

I went to her mother the next day and asked her if she saw Shemika and if she could keep Calvin, until her daughter comes to get him, because I had to go to work. Ms. Sarah told me no. That she already raised her children, that she wasn't raising another child. She told me to go to her other daughter, Abbigail and ask her to keep Calvin and she told me no, that she and Shemika didn't get along and that Shemika does that kind of thing all the time and eventually she would turn up.

I had to contact CPS and the police and they were going to take Calvin and put him in the system. I couldn't bear to watch Calvin grow up in the system, so I stepped out on faith and raised Calvin, along with my mother's help. I became his foster mother and later, I was able to adopt him.

I want you all to know if my son Calvin was just a regular student, with decent grades and you never saw him in the papers or on all the news channels, then I promise you, we wouldn't be here. But because my son has a bright future ahead of him and is going into the NBA when he graduates, my so called best friend and her mother is seeing dollar signs, flashing in front of their eyes right now. They think this will be their come up from where they're at because Calvin will take care of them and give them money.

This is only about money. This is the only reason why we're here in the first place. How in the world a mother can give her child to her best friend to watch for a few hours that night and never come back? And to have the freaking nerve, after being gone for sixteen years, accuse me of kidnapping my son, when all I did was raise him and love him. All the things a real mother is supposed to do for her child. Shemika, you may be his biological mother, but you are definitely not his mother. I'm his mother, today, tomorrow and forever.

Everything my son needed, I had to provide it for him. Food, a roof over his head, clothes on his back, I paid for it, while putting myself through college. I earned my nursing degree, while my mother helped me with Calvin, so I could provide for him. I wanted to give my son, yes my son, a good life, while his biological mother was out there either strung out on drugs, somewhere drunk, or lying up with some man or men. Just living the life while I was left to take her responsibility that became my responsibility because her own family didn't want to take him in.

Now Shemika comes in after sixteen years, almost seventeen years of this boy's life and said I kidnapped him, and I lost three months of my life and my son's life because I was locked up for nothing. What's going to happen to her judge? How much time is she going to get for wasting this court's time? Making me lose time from work, being humiliated while the police came to my job and arrested me for something I didn't do. What is she going to get? She deserves a lot more for the hell I had to go through.

Shemika, you are some piece of work and your mother had the audacity to sit right here and act like she didn't know I had Calvin. I guess the apple doesn't fall far from the tree huh? Shemika, I'm ashamed of you. I regret the day I ever met you and uttered those words of calling you my friend. You should be ashamed of yourself and I hope you rot in hell for everything you have done. Trust me, you will get all this back," I said, as I wiped my tears for the last time. I was done shedding tears over this individual that I thought was my friend, that was only there to use me and now I see that, when I couldn't all before.

"Ms. Martin, I'm so sorry for everything that young lady put you through and it is so obvious that your mother raised you right for you to have done a fantastic job raising your son. You're right, that young lady has caused you a lot of pain but believe me, she won't cause you anymore pain after today. Ms. Martin, continue to live your best life and I wish you and your son a wonderful life. You may step down," the judge said.

I stepped down, with a sense of pride and for a long time, I felt like I was finally getting my life back together and I was ready to put all the hell that I've been through with walking away from an abusing, toxic marriage, to losing my mother and Mrs. Ollie Mae, to being arrested for something that I didn't do, and now losing a friend that was never really a friend to me in the first place. I was ready to close this chapter of my life and move on.

"Stand up young lady," the judge told Shemika. Shemika stood up, acting like she was too ashamed to look at the judge. "Ma'am, you have really wasted this court's time by filing these bogus, false allegations against this young lady. It seems like you enjoy staying and walking away from the people that care and love you so I'm going to have you do that again for another ten years.

I sentence you to ten years in the women's prison in Columbia, South Carolina. This will give you plenty of time to think about your actions and everything you've done to this young lady as well as your son. Ma'am, I hope one day you learn how to be a true friend because right now, it seems like you have no idea of the meaning of the word. Officers, please take her away now," the Judge said.

The officers placed the handcuffs on Shemika and she started screaming. "I'm sorry Tammy! I'm sorry Calvin! I don't know what came over me! I was being selfish! Please don't let them take me!" Shemika yelled, as they took her away.

I turned to Lawrence and hugged him tightly. "Thank you so much Lawrence for everything. I owe you big time," I said. "You certainly do. Just have a great life and be happy with you and your son," Lawrence said. "I will and thank you again," I said, as I turned to head out the door.

Calvin ran up to me and hugged me. "Mom, please forgive me for how I treated you. I should've never thought that you would ever kidnap me from my mother. I know I should be ashamed of myself, for doubting you," Calvin said. "Don't worry about it son, this case had us all thinking and believing all kinds of crazy things," I said, hugging Calvin and kissing him on the cheek.

I was so overwhelmed that I couldn't stay mad at my son, even if I wanted to. I was just so thankful for being out of jail and getting back to my normal life again, that I didn't have time to be angry at anyone. "Mom, this is Tina, my girlfriend," Calvin said. "Hello. Nice to meet you Tina," I said, shaking the young lady's hand. I didn't particularly care for Calvin inviting Tina to my court hearing like that, allowing her to meet me after seeing me on trial, for something I didn't do, giving her a bad impression of me before she got to know me, but I swear sometimes Calvin really doesn't think at all.

I shook my head because I knew that was just a part of him and if he hasn't changed his way of thinking in seventeen years, I know he wasn't going to start now. As I was walking out, I saw Tim walking out of the courtroom, along with his wife, judging by the way she had her arm tucked under his arm. I knew exactly who his wife was. It was Lisa, from my jail cell, that was trying to get up in my business. I guess they wanted to see if I really did kidnap Calvin and they were using her as a decoy to get information out of me. I knew I couldn't trust her and I was right.

I only wish my judgment was that good when I decided on the day I met my so called best friend Shemika, and ran far away from her or when I met my ex-husband, and knew he wasn't the man for me. Where was this good judgment at then? I guess time and maturity will give you growth and understanding, and that's exactly what I got.

Lisa waved at me as she walked out of the courtroom with Timothy. I just shook my head at her. "Mom, let me get you home," Calvin said. "That sounds good son," I said. As I walked out of the building, I heard someone call my name. I turned around and saw it was Ms. Sarah, calling me.

I wanted to stick my middle finger at that woman and tell her to get her conniving, lying behind away from me but I wanted to see what she had to say. Ms. Sarah walked up to me. "Tamara, I'm so sorry for everything. I know I got up there and lied about everything, trying to make you look bad but I guess everything worked out in your favor," Ms. Sarah said. "Yes it did. You can't hold a good woman down. Not even you or your lying behind daughter can do that. I see exactly where Shemika gets it from. My mother always said, that Shemika was no true friend to me because she was just like you and I see exactly what she meant. Take care of yourself Ms. Sarah, I have a feeling, you're going to get all this right back on you," I said, as I walked out of the courthouse and got in Calvin's car.

As Calvin drove out of the courthouse parking lot, I knew this was a day I wanted to put far behind me. They say God doesn't put more on us then we can bear but I had no idea how God thought I would be able to bear this, because this was something that almost made me lose my mind. But God held me together through it all. "Thank you God for keeping my mind in the midst of all of this. Amen."

Chapter 35

Thank You Mom

I RETURNED BACK TO WORK LAST week and of course everyone was so happy to see me. Pam hugged me so tightly and told me she didn't believe for one second that I could ever kidnap anyone and she was so glad that I was cleared of all charges. I thanked Pam for everything and for her trust in me. I told Pam after the three months that I had, I needed some time from work. I told her I needed to take a short leave of absence, just to get myself together and to spend time with Calvin before his graduation. Pam told me she certainly understood.

Pam told me when I returned, we have to discuss a new position she wanted to offer me. She was being promoted to a Nurse Administrator and she wanted to offer me the Nursing Director position. I told Pam that I would definitely discuss that when I return because I didn't want to make a rash decision right now. She agreed that we could talk more about it when I returned from my time away.

I got dressed and I couldn't believe that my baby was graduating high school today. Where has the time gone? I so wish Mom was here to help celebrate this day with us. Mom would be so proud of Calvin to not only see her one and only grandchild walk across that stage to get his diploma, but to see him get his associate's degree in business and to be graduating as his class valedictorian as well, with a 4.3 GPA.

I couldn't stop smiling and crying all morning, thinking about Calvin. Calvin told me at first he didn't want to march for graduation and that he might let them mail him his diploma and degree. I almost rung Calvin's neck when he said that. I told him he was marching and he wasn't about to take that moment from me of watching my only child walk across that stage. Calvin told me he wouldn't dare take that moment from me.

Calvin has been nervous all day about his valedictorian speech he has to give at graduation. He told me he had no idea what he wanted to say to all his fellow classmates as they depart into the world to start their new lives. I told Calvin that God will give him the words just as long as he says them from his heart. Calvin nodded his head and told me he was definitely going to do that.

I know my baby has truly been through a lot that most young men his age, wouldn't be able to take but he managed to outshine everything. After Shemika went to prison, she couldn't take it and ended up killing herself. They said she asked for a pencil to write a letter and when the guard gave it to her, she took it back to her cell, wrapped herself up in her sheet and stabbed herself in the neck with it and by the time the officers did their two-hour count, they found her dead in her bed.

I knew Shemika wasn't cut out for prison so her killing herself really didn't surprise me at all. I asked Calvin how he felt about what Shemika did and of course he told me he couldn't feel anything for someone he didn't know but he was sorry to know she killed herself. He asked me if he should feel bad for feeling that way; I told Calvin he couldn't help how he felt and besides that, he didn't know her.

They had a small service for Shemika at their church and I didn't go. I didn't want to stand over her grave, knowing I didn't truly forgive her for how she tried to wreck my life so I figured it was best if I stayed home. I told Calvin he was more than welcome to go but he didn't want to go either. I told him I was going to let that be his decision, whether he wanted to go or not.

I finished curling my hair and grabbing my things to head to graduation. Calvin left two hours ago still nervous, but happy at the same time. I can't believe this day has come. I headed out the door, trying to hold myself together. I swear if someone had told me I would be a mother about to watch my son graduate, I wouldn't believe them, especially when the odds were against me for being able to be a parent.

I walked in the gym, thinking about that day that I lost my baby when I was seventeen years old, and the doctors gave that horrible news that nearly knocked me off my feet, when they said I won't ever be able to bear children. I swear, the way I screamed in that hospital, you would've thought that the doctor told me I had a few hours to live, the way I reacted that day.

I wondered how life could be so cruel to me for me to miscarry and then to find out that I wouldn't be able to bear any children for as long as I live. The doctors may have said that but God had other plans. Shemika might have had terrible intentions of leaving Calvin with me that night, when she said she was coming back, but if she didn't I would've never experienced how it would feel to be a mother to Calvin.

I wouldn't know how to love this little person that was looking for love and looking at me with desperation in his eyes, looking for someone to love him. I knew what he was looking for because I wanted that same kind of love too. I had the love of my mother and father but I wanted it from my own child. My child to look up at me, and call me "Mom," and love me and not see any fault in me. I may not be perfect by any means, but I tried my best to be a good person and a good mother to Calvin.

I don't drink, or have I ever done any drugs. I didn't stay in the streets, running behind a man, acting like I needed this and needed that. Calvin needed a mother to look up to and respect. He needed someone that he could hold accountable to, because when he got out of hand or out of control, I had to show him tough love and discipline, because if I didn't do it as his mother, I definitely didn't want anyone else doing it, like the police officers or teachers, because I failed to do what I had to do as a parent.

I knew that I had to be a mother to my son and not his friend because he would have plenty of friends in life growing up but he only gets one mother and I needed to be that for him. I just hope I was a good mother to him like my mother were to me.

As they called all the high school graduates names, I stood up clapping for every student but when they called Calvin Martin's name, I couldn't keep my composure as I screamed out loud, as loud as I could, "That's my son! That's my baby! You did it Son!" I couldn't stop the tears and the excitement as everyone was looking at me.

"You go right ahead and scream for your son. I'm sure he knows just how proud you are of him," a little older black lady said beside me. I smiled and nodded my head. "Thank you," I replied.

The principal Mr. Lewis came to the podium to acknowledge Calvin. "Ladies and gentlemen, I want to present to you this year's valedictorian Mr. Calvin Martin. He is an exceptional young man with a 4.3 GPA and an excellent basketball player. As a matter of fact, he will be drafted into the NBA this coming year October as a first-time draft pick for the LA. Lakers.

I am so proud of this young man for his hard work and his dedication here at Manning High School. Calvin, you will do great work and I'm so proud to be your principal. Continue to make us proud," Mr. Lewis said, as he hugged Calvin and shook his hand.

Calvin came to the podium and paused. I could tell my son was full of emotions and needed that minute to get himself together. "Hello ladies, gentlemen, parents, staff members, school officials and to my fellow classmates of 2024. Today is the day that the Lord has made and let us rejoice in it. I want to acknowledge God who is the head of my life, and my beautiful mother who has been by my side through it all. Mom, where are you? Please stand up and wave your hand," Calvin said.

I stood up and waved my hand and they immediately had me on the camera on all the projector screens. I've never been one to like the spotlight but this time, I'm making the exception since this is my only baby and today is his big day. "I want to thank my mother for always being there for me and being by my side the entire time. I'm sure many of you all know the story that was recently surfaced about my birth and my alleged kidnapping, which wasn't true and I'm ashamed to say, that I didn't know what to believe because I was also more involved in what the news and tabloids were saying, than trusting and believing with my own heart, that my mother would never do what she was accused of.

My mother was found innocent and I felt horrible for not believing her when she first told me she didn't do it. I'm saying that because that little testimony is a part of my speech that I titled, "Listen to that voice, that will never steer you wrong."

I stood up the entire time in tears, while Calvin said his speech because my son was no longer talking and speaking, he was preaching his trial sermon because I definitely felt like I was in church and not only was I the only one standing up, but everyone around me was standing up as well. "I don't know your son, but the way how that young man talked about you, and thanked you, I could tell you're a great mother," a white lady said on the other side of me. "Thank you so much," I said.

Calvin said he doesn't know what he would do without me, because I kept him from going to foster care and I saved his life but he doesn't know that he saved my life as well. He helped heal a broken person that really didn't know how heartbroken, and lonely I was until he came into my life. Thank you God for my precious gift, my son.

The End

By John D. McCray

www.ingramcontent.com/pod-product-compliance
Lightning Source LLC
Chambersburg PA
CBHW021625120626
46545CB00002B/408